# PETER FABER

# PETER FABER

## a saint for turbulent times

Jon M. Sweeney

LOYOLA PRESS.
A JESUIT MINISTRY
Chicago

LOYOLA PRESS.
A JESUIT MINISTRY

3441 N. Ashland Avenue
Chicago, Illinois 60657
(800) 621-1008
www.loyolapress.com

Author photo: Maury Woll, Cover art: ziggymaj/Digital Visions Vectors/Getty Images, Gary Kelly, Potapov Alexander/Shutterstock, 123ducu/iStock/Getty Images, The Crosiers/Gene Plaisted, OSC.

ISBN: 978-0-8294-4522-0
Library of Congress Control Number: 2020939167

Printed in the United States of America.

20 21 22 23 24 25 26 27 28 29 Versa 10 9 8 7 6 5 4 3 2 1

*Master Pierre says he has no wish to have zeal for the execution of God's justice . . . but only zeal for mercy.*[1]

—"Teachings of Pierre Favre"


*His was . . . a restless, unsettled spirit that was never satisfied.*[2]

—Pope Francis, speaking about Peter Faber

# Contents

# Author's Note

I couldn't find Peter Faber anywhere. After reading reminiscences and letters of St. Ignatius of Loyola and also the life of St. Francis Xavier—the two recognized stars among the founding members of the Society of Jesus—it was almost as if Faber hadn't existed. Even a new textbook of primary sources from the founding generation, *Jesuit Writings of the Early Modern Period*, yielded nothing.[3]

But more than a few Jesuit friends had said to me over the years that Faber was the one to whom they most often turned for guidance and inspiration. "He's my favorite Jesuit," one said. "Faber represents the real heart of what it all means," said another.

So, why was it so hard to find him? How had he slipped away unnoticed from the history of those formative years in Europe? Why does he play such a small part in the early histories of the Jesuits? I knew the Society of Jesus was founded by three men—Ignatius, Xavier, and Peter Faber—at a time when Christians seemed to be at one another's throats. The four decades of Faber's life coincided with the world reinventing itself.

Geographically, Columbus had just inaugurated transatlantic navigation, opening avenues to conquest and colonization for European powers. Four years earlier, the Portuguese nobleman Bartholomew Diaz had rounded the Cape of Good Hope (the southernmost tip of Africa), passing from the mighty Atlantic to the Indian Ocean. This was how Faber's friend, Xavier, was to travel to India, Japan, and China, following on the heels and vessels of the Kingdom of Portugal, the first of the colonial empires.

Politically, nations were aligning along religious lines, as there were suddenly more churches in the West than just Roman Catholic ones, and additional authorities in the church besides the pope. Protestant (the word comes from *protest*) reformers had emerged a century earlier in outlying regions of the Holy Roman Empire in the form of the English preacher John Wycliffe and the Bohemian priest Jan Hus. By the time Faber was a teenager, German princes felt emboldened to support a young friar-theologian, Martin Luther, in his disputes with the Catholic Church and to declare a national church in Germany to challenge Rome. Wherever there was significant interest and intervention by political leaders, the Reformation tended to succeed.[4]

Theologically, the Reformation was a dam that had loosed dangerous waters.

It was only half a century later when scientists, philosophers, and other churchmen felt empowered to question more than what Luther had challenged. Luther stuck to church matters, such as the meaning of sacraments and the value of priests. Fifty years later, though, others questioned the actual tentpoles of who we are and what life is about. The earth ceased to be understood as at the center of the universe (Giordano Bruno). The heavens were no longer unchanging or perfect (Galileo Galilei). And new means of pursuing knowledge declared every appeal to authority in such matters to be invalid (René Descartes, then others).

A door had closed. The medieval era had ended. Full stop.

The Society of Jesus was there while all this happened: Francis Xavier as one of the early sixteenth century's trailblazing explorers and missionaries, and Ignatius of Loyola as one of that era's most influential figures involved in buttressing a teetering Christendom. But what about Peter Faber? I wanted to find the saint that people talked about, who was so important to the Jesuits and yet so unknown to the story of those times.

Then, during my search, on November 24, 2013, Pope Francis announced that he was canonizing this obscure sixteenth-century priest by means of "equivalent canonization." This unusual way of "making a saint" means that the pope dispenses with some of the usual requirements and judicial procedures associated with the process. He can do so only if it is clear there's been a constant devotion to the person among the faithful, if historians have consistently attested to the character and virtue of the subject, and if there has been a steady stream of wonders and miracles associated with the subject's intercession. Pope Francis made clear that he and many others have long had a most sincere devotion to the new saint, "a man," the pope said, "capable of great and strong decisions but also capable of being so gentle and loving."[5] As it turned out, Pope Francis was one of those Jesuits who had a profound devotion to the most obscure of the founding three. When he characterized Faber by saying, "[He] was consumed by the intense desire to communicate the Lord. If we do not have his same desire, then we need to pause in prayer, and, with silent fervor, ask the Lord, through the intercession of our brother Peter, to return and attract us. Pope Francis revealed that he modeled himself after 'that fascination with the Lord that led Peter to such apostolic folly.'"[6]

So, Faber, who had seemed to have been lost in the most turbulent, violent, and formative century in the history of the West, was found once again, at least in Rome.

Previous biographies of Peter Faber, with good and pious intentions, have pointed to testimonies given during 1598 hearings for Faber's beatification (he *did* make it that far four centuries ago) that made him out to be a simple boy of blessed disposition who grew to be a saintly man. His mind was always preoccupied with holy matters, the testimonies said, with stories of the young Faber precociously instructing others, like Christ in the temple, except that Peter was apparently just six or seven years old. Even the rock upon which the boy sat while sermonizing was remembered and commemorated. It was said that he fasted at times when others did not, and, who knows, perhaps he did, because children caught up in religious fervor are often the most dramatically ardent in shows of devotion. Then, when he was just ten, "a desire began to burn in his pure soul with the intensity of the evening star in a clear sky."[7]

These accounts could never satisfy the inquiries of a mind seeking the real Faber. I wanted to find this figure for myself, and I've come to the search with the questions of one who sincerely loves the saints but also with the questions of a twenty-first-century person. In the process of looking, reading, and thinking, what I have discovered surprised me and left me wondering what might have been different in the turbulent sixteenth century if Faber had lived longer—or if his lead had been followed.

To follow Faber and tell his tale, we will travel to many countries in Europe. Who he was is not easy to pin down or define. For example, consider his names. Born French, as Pierre Favre, halfway between Geneva and the Italian Po River valley, he spent the second half of his life traveling almost constantly, from Portugal to Spain to Germany to Italy and back again. But sometimes he wrote letters in Spanish, signing his name Fabro. Today, we know him as Faber, the Latinized version of his name, which was surely how he began spelling it when he arrived at university. These cosmopolitan qualities make him seem a bit like the most popular Catholic spiritual writer of the twentieth century, the Trappist monk Thomas Merton, who was born in France, then educated in England, lived mostly in Middle America, and passed away while traveling throughout the Far East. As someone who has studied Merton and found that his international identity is a key to seeing him as he was, I would say the same is true for understanding Faber.

Then, as is true for every pivotal figure in history, there are supporting characters to consider in his life story. There are many who come in and out of the frame. These include soldiers and sons, bishops and monks, queens and maidens, firebrand reformers and restless prophets. This story includes accounts of feuds and bloodshed, of writers at their desks, patients in recuperating rooms, friends lost in cities, and priests accompanying princesses on journeys. Even the French Revolution plays a part in this story.

And just because Faber's story is history doesn't mean that it is not important for today. There is a timeliness to this search for him, especially since Pope Francis declared that Faber is his favorite saint after Francis of Assisi. The holy pontiff has praised Faber's "restlessness" and "dreaming," which is curious, given that these are foolish qualities by any worldly standard. Faber wasn't a simple man, and this is no simple hagiography. Many people during his lifetime thought he was a fool for believing that he could forge an intimacy with God and that, by love and friendship, he could heal the differences between people that were causing them not just to separate and fight but also to hurt and kill each other. Perhaps he was a fool, but if so, he was a fool for God in a distinguished line of Christian tradition. That also means, by most worldly standards, that his life would be considered a failure.

There are ways in which coming to see who Faber really was points us in new and helpful ways toward a more authentic life with God and more authentic relationships with others. For all these reasons, this is much more than armchair travel and history. This search for Faber might even show us what is possible in our own day. Particularly, if Pope Francis is right, this story could show us how we are able to continue the story of Faber in our lives today.

# The Overture

This is the story of the life of Peter Faber, but it is more than that. It's an account of how Faber and his companions came to answer the most basic questions in life: Who are we? What is life about? And, how can we understand ourselves?

Human beings are difficult to understand. We have trouble contemplating ourselves, let alone one another. How many close friends, siblings, and spouses have come to the end of a long life together with someone they love, only to realize that they hardly knew that friend, brother or sister, husband or wife, at all?

What makes each of us unique? If I press friends with this nonrhetorical question, answers range from body parts (faces, smiles, gaits) to the metaphysically intangible (spirit). No one responds by saying that their hands or hair or lips are the thing that makes them unique, even if they tend these things carefully. No one I've ever asked has identified keenly with their kidneys, fingers, or feet. Most people say that their mind is what makes them unique. Perhaps their brain. Or their "heart."

What a difference five centuries make. In Faber's era, there was no functioning of a mind without the work of a soul. The answer to the question of what makes a person unique would have been nearly unanimous: the soul.

*Psyche* and *Geist* mean both "soul" and "mind" in ancient Greek and modern German. They are one and the same. Similarly, *nous*, or "reason," in Plato and the writings of the church fathers is essentially mental and spiritual perception together, at once. For those ancient masters, this is what our mind does: intuit, feel, think, and understand in every aspect of our lives. So, whether 2,500 years ago, when Plato was teaching, or 500 years ago, when the Society of Jesus began, people have understood the mind and the soul as dependent on each other. I believe they still are.

Faber understood this as well. We wouldn't be able to find him or understand his life without first grasping this essential teaching of the founding members of the Society of Jesus. What makes a person unique? Answering that question was their lives' work. A century ago, Sigmund Freud said, "In the future science will go beyond religion, and reason will replace faith in God." It's become abundantly clear how wrong he was. One has only to read the daily headlines to see how wrong they were who predicted the demise of faith. Science has taught religion a great many things, but that prophesied and hoped-for replacement never happened, and as it turns out, the revelatory way that Faber and his friends began to describe the meaning of the human person revolutionized psychology.

Faber, Ignatius, and Xavier inherited an understanding of spiritual psychology from the classics of their university education. One of these classics was established 250 years before Faber was born, when Thomas Aquinas at the University of Paris assigned the human faculty of reason to the soul.

*Anima* is the Latin word for soul, and it is also the Latin translation of the Greek word *psyche*. For Thomas Aquinas, the soul was not a religious component of people; it was the animating principle of the human body itself. It would take philosophers such as Hume and Kant, after Faber's time, to begin to deny spiritual perception and treat reason as a function purely of a calculating machine that atomists knew as the brain; hence, human reason becomes, for Hume, "the slave of the passions." In response, Kant rehabilitates the possibility of a limited form of rationality, but still without soul.

Since the philosophers took hatchets to St. Thomas's ideas, our forebears have understood their souls in ways that we have, since then, only been familiar with our minds. I hear priests today lamenting the lack of biblical and theological literacy among members of their congregations. "They don't read or inquire, as we once did," they say. When I hear this, I think of how much they—and all of us—are missing. I don't think a lack of curiosity and learning is our problem. People look, see, and absorb more information than ever before. The problem is that we've lost sight of our souls. Where does all the information go? What good is knowledge without the soul to receive and grasp it?

Faber, Ignatius, and Xavier would soon help millions of people come to understand more than the philosophical question of how a soul animates the body. It was Faber and friends who renewed (from Bernard of Clairvaux, from Francis of Assisi) in Christian teaching insights and practices such as the following:

- The defeating power that negative emotions have in our lives
- The power of the imagination in experiencing the life of Christ
- The importance of taking time each day to pause and examine our actions and decisions, for example, asking oneself, *Why did I do that?*
- Giving thanks, showing gratitude, for things big and small
- Spiritual direction: looking to a counselor, friend, mentor, or priest to whom we may confide and be completely honest
- Listening to our emotions: learning to discern, daily, what makes us feel sad, what is upsetting, what brings us happiness, and why

How we understand who we are changed because of what Faber and friends would create: a process for plumbing the soul that no one had fully attempted or experienced before. It would come to be called, deceptively simply, Spiritual Exercises. It would be nearly a century before they ever bothered to publish these exercises as a book, even though they lived during a time when every religious figure with half an opinion was lining up to run off copies of his book, broadsheet, or poster on the era's revolutionary new tool, the printing press.

The Exercises—in the early days, they were often known in shorthand as simply the Exercises—began with Iñigo. That is the name by which we will know Ignatius of Loyola in part 1 of this book. The inner life of human beings was Iñigo's textbook, and he crafted the Exercises from his own experience. Then he realized that no spiritual exercises are best done alone. A "soul friend," as Iñigo came to call it, or companion—a spiritual director—is required. Many people misunderstand this requirement today or disregard it altogether. But Iñigo knew, as the desert fathers and mothers and other Christian mystics knew before him, that it can be dangerous to undergo intense spiritual practice and interiority on one's own. Never mind that it can be literally dangerous to approach the living God; those who have been there understand what often accompanies the stages of a serious spiritual quest: depression, despairing thoughts, even suicidal tendencies. A woman or man for whom all is "fine" does not usually take such a journey. Moses, Daniel, John the Baptist, Paul, Antony, and Hildegard—these were all people on some sort of edge. Only those who realize the needs of their soul will pursue a relationship with God. After Iñigo showed these new Exercises to Faber, they became Faber's personal passion, field of research, and vocation, as well. Faber in fact became their most adept teacher.

In a time when religious understandings of the soul went mostly unchallenged, the Spiritual Exercises opened the potential for human psychology. Its impact for contemplating and expanding the inner life wouldn't be matched until the advent of psychoanalysis 350 years later, when psychoanalysts seemed to believe they had discovered it.

Only when organized religion began to lose its influence over our lives did science step in. That period in history began, as we will see, during Faber's own lifetime. This is part of the personal disappointment one discovers in the search for Faber: his own feelings of loss. However, imaginative contemplation, the Spiritual Exercises' gift to human understanding, continues to have a huge influence on what we know about the soul. This is just one more way in which Faber's story is about more than him, or his life and times; it is also about the search to find what makes us truly human and to know how that humanness connects us to God.

# Basic Chronology of Peter Faber's Life

| | |
|---|---|
| April 13, 1506 | Born in the Duchy of Savoy, in the mountains of southeastern France, bordering Italy and Switzerland. |
| September 1516 | Begs his parents to send him to school, as he is tired of shepherding and passionate about learning; they acquiesce. |
| October 31, 1517 | The Augustinian friar Martin Luther nails his Ninety-Five Theses, or protests against Catholic Church doctrine and practice, on the door of the Wittenberg church in Germany, sending shock waves throughout Christendom. |
| September 1525 | Walks with companions 350 miles north of his home, across the mountains, to attend the Collège Sainte-Barbe at the University of Paris. Meets Francis Xavier, his first roommate. |
| September 1529 | Meets Ignatius of Loyola, who joins Faber and Xavier, sharing rooms at university together. They all become close friends, even though Ignatius is fourteen years older. |
| 1530 | Earns his master of arts degree. |
| May 30, 1534 | Ordained a priest. |
| August 15, 1534 | Takes permanent vows with six others as a founding member of what becomes the Society of Jesus. |
| Summer 1535–Winter 1536 | Temporary leader of the band of vowed brothers. Journeys with the others to Venice, in preparation for journeying to Palestine. |
| Lent–September 1539 | Meets regularly with the other original Jesuits to write "The Formula of the Institute," or the Rule, of their new religious order. Pope Paul III gives his oral approval to the group on September 3, saying, "The Spirit of God is here."[a] |
| September 27, 1540 | Pope Paul III's papal bull grants formal approval to the Society. |
| October 1540—April 1541 | Attends the Colloquy of Worms and the Diet of Regensburg in Germany, the latter presided over by Emperor Charles V; attempts to reconcile Protestants and Catholics. |

| January 1542—1543 | Travels throughout cities in Germany meeting with church leaders, engaging reformers, and seeking to reconcile factions. |
| --- | --- |
| 1544–45 | Preaches throughout Portugal and Spain, becoming friends with Francis Borgia, the future superior general of the Society of Jesuits, and King John III of Portugal. |
| April 1546 | Begins journey from Portugal toward the north of Italy after Pope Paul III asks him to represent the Holy See at the Council of Trent. |
| August 1, 1546 | Dies in Rome, in the arms of his friend Ignatius of Loyola. |
| a. Antonio M. de Aldama, SJ, *The Formula of the Institute: Notes for a Commentary* (St. Louis, MO: Institute for Jesuit Sources, 1990), 30. ||

# Principal Characters

## Three friends in Paris

**Peter Faber,** the sensitive son of farmers in the Savoy Alps, who learns to pray while shepherding and then desires something more. He finds that something more in Paris at university, and by meeting Ignatius of Loyola, then spends his relatively short life traveling all over Europe to teach others how to do likewise. This is his story.

**Francis Xavier,** royal born in the Kingdom of Navarre, on Spain's northern border with France, Faber's contemporary, whose life irrevocably changes at age nine when his father dies and his older brothers lose a fight to repel forces of the Spanish king. Family wealth and property are confiscated, and Francis leaves for Paris. There, at nineteen, he becomes Peter's roommate in Paris. Later, he becomes one of the most intrepid and important Christian missionaries since the apostle Paul.

**Ignatius "Iñigo" Loyola**, a proud but wounded Basque gentleman-soldier, fourteen years older than Xavier and Peter Faber, whom he meets at the University of Paris. They form a triumvirate that transforms Europe and the Catholic Church. He authors a book about the process of religious imagination and formation called *Spiritual Exercises*. It is Iñigo who first teaches Faber, in Faber's words, "how to get to know myself and discern God's will."

## Reformers

**Martin Bucer,** a French Dominican who is convinced to annul his vows after meeting and hearing Martin Luther. He becomes a preacher and teacher throughout France before retiring to England. For a time, Bucer and Faber meet frequently at colloquies arranged by Charles V to reconcile Catholics and Protestants. Bucer and Faber were early ecumenists.

**Martin Luther,** the German Augustinian friar and professor of theology who publicly protests the abuse of indulgences (remission of temporal punishment due for sin, even after absolution) with his famous posting of the Ninety-Five Theses of disagreement with the Catholic Church on the door of the church in Wittenberg, Germany. This happens when Faber is eleven. Luther then formally separates from the church four years before Faber leaves for university in Paris. Pope Leo X excommunicates Luther, and Faber dreams of bringing Luther back to the fold.

**Philipp Melanchthon,** Luther's young lieutenant, later his spiritual and denominational heir, and a man with an even greater taste for theological battle

## Other Luminaries

**Charles V,** Holy Roman Emperor, a Catholic, but one who wants to unite his kingdom and knows that religion is forever dividing it. Convener of the Colloquy of Worms and the Diet of Regensburg, both of which fail in their objective.

**Pope Paul III,** the Holy Father who nurtures Faber and other first members of the Society of Jesus. Paul III's election takes place two months after the original seven of them take their first vows; he formally approves them as a religious order six years later. Today, his papacy is usually defined by the Counter-Reformation, when the Catholic Church labored to redefine itself in the midst of the Protestant revolt, but during most of his papacy he was trying to find a way to keep the church together.

**Princess Maria Manuela,** the eldest daughter of King John III of Portugal, engaged to be married to Philip II, the future king of Spain. Faber is asked to accompany her from Lisbon to Salamanca for the ceremony.

**Francis Borgia,** hereditary duke of Gandía, in Spain, and member of the infamous Borgia family. Born into incredible wealth, he was the grandson of the philandering Pope Alexander VI, schooled in the court of Holy Roman Emperor Charles V, Francis Borgia's wife dies the same summer Faber dies. Borgia quickly joins the Society of Jesus, easing its formal acceptance by the papacy, eventually becoming its third superior general and one of its saints.

# PART ONE

# 1

## Down in the Mountains

*We begin life in a very odd manner—like shipwrecked sailors.*[8]
—Lytton Strachey

### 1506—1525

Leo Tolstoy's novel *Anna Karenina* begins with the sentence, "Happy families are all alike; every unhappy family is unhappy in its own way." Peter Faber came from a sincerely happy family. His childhood appears, at least on the surface, to have been idyllic in many of the ways all happy families are unremarkable. At the same time, he appears to have had little interest in remaining simply happy.

He had a loving mother and a caring father, Marie and Louis, as well as two brothers, Louis and John. They lived a pastoral existence together near the River Borne in the mountain hamlet of Villaret, in the diocese of Geneva, in the Duchy of Savoy, where Faber was born on April 13, 1506. It was an Easter Monday, and it is said his parents took no chances: they baptized him that same evening at their parish church of Saint-Jean-de-Sixt. This village lies in the Aravis Range of mountains in the French Alps—to the immediate west of the tallest of the Alps, which are in Italy. Saint-Jean-de-Sixt is situated only a few miles from the eastern border of France. Little could the infant Peter have known what turmoil the world around him was in just then.

In England, a a young man who would become Henry VIII was already married to Catherine of Aragon and preparing to be king. The English believed that their monarchy, as well as their long-term security, was in good hands. A male heir was surely soon on his way.

In Germany, a twenty-three-year-old Martin Luther was a novice friar in the Augustinian order, training to become a priest. After earning his master of arts and beginning law school, he then experienced a dramatic religious conversion and abandoned those plans, instead entering the Reformed Congregation of the Eremetical Order of St. Augustine at Erfurt, in central Germany. Despite his father's objections, Luther was intending to apply his fiery talents to serving the Roman Catholic Church.

And in Rome, just two months before Faber was born, the great Michelangelo had convinced Pope Julius II to put a life-size sculpture of Laocoön and his twin sons, Antiphas and Thymbraeus (all legendary figures of Greek and Roman mythology), being crushed to death by two sea serpents, on public display in the Vatican. This ancient work of art had just been unearthed in a vineyard nearby, outside the church of Santa Maria Maggiore. Educated people in every city of Christendom were talking about it. Julius II was a classicist pope sitting in St. Peter's Chair, and what we know now as "the Renaissance" was then in full flower. When Faber was two years old, Michelangelo would begin painting the ceiling of the Sistine Chapel. By Faber's fifth birthday, Julius II had laid the foundation stone for the new St. Peter's Basilica.

All over Europe, cities were gaining in importance as people left rural places to find new opportunities. Serfdom was about to end in most corners of the continent but not all. Heresy was sparking in churches, and occasionally, heretical tyrants were in control of whole cities until or unless they were squashed. And piles of money were being donated and raised, by indulgences and other means, for that great project of Pope Julius: the design and construction of St. Peter's Basilica in Rome. Money was a problem in the church in other ways too. For example, simony—the buying and selling of ecclesiastical privileges—was common. Albert of Brandenburg, a son of noble parents, made his profession in the church, with high ambition. When Albert discovered that he had to pay Rome ten thousand ducats to obtain a coveted cardinal's hat, he hired John Tetzel to sell indulgences throughout Germany so he could cover the cost. It was Tetzel who would soon infuriate young Luther.

None of these things, however, was happening in sleepy little Villaret, but Faber likely heard talk of them among travelers, soldiers, and pilgrims. One of the most magnetic of pilgrimage destinations of that era lay just to the west: the French bishopric commune of Le Puy (today's Le Puy-en-Velay), a place considered nearly as holy in those times as the Holy Land itself. Famous relics, including a Black Virgin, were in the cathedral in Le Puy, and popes, emperors, and kings—from Charlemagne in the year 800 through to every French king for several hundred years after him—came there seeking blessings. Faber surely dreamed of taking this journey himself one day. It wasn't far. Meanwhile, his little French alpine hamlet was very quiet.

By the River Borne, day after day, the happy Faber family rose early, worked hard, took their meals together, and observed the seasons of the year as families in any good farming community would. Peter's parents filled their table with good food: boiled eggs, pumpkin soup, bowls of pears, rabbits, and partridges. Faber sat in the mountain valleys day by day, a shepherd watching sheep, dreaming. By all accounts, the Fabers were pious, religiously observant folk, and the children were encouraged to learn their catechism. Their mother told them stories of Our Lady.

To Faber, these pious activities took on a different life than they did for his brothers, Louis and John. Peter had the uncanny ability to remember everything he read or heard. His mother had to say something only once. And his gift wasn't only for memorization: his imagination was also more vivid than that of others. Stories of the Annunciation or of walking with Our Lord by the Sea of Galilee became more real to Faber than even the cornflowers he saw in the fields each day. This capacity for imagination would prepare and serve him well later for life as a member of the Society of Jesus.

Peter's parents were dear to him in their happy home. As an adult, Faber credits the faith of his father and mother, the religious instruction he received from them, and God's grace with teaching him to be a witness to his own sinfulness, mild as it must have been, by the age of seven. "I began," he later wrote in his spiritual memoir, "while still very young, to be aware of myself."[9] By this, he meant that he was grateful they taught him the fear of the Lord.

Also, from a young age, his daily work was that of a shepherd. The Fabers lived amid the Aravis Range of the French Prealps: subalpine, mostly limestone, mountains to the immediate west of the towering French and Italian

Alps. It is a stunningly beautiful place. Today, the nearby Le Grand-Bornand village attracts tourists for hiking, skiing, rock climbing, and paragliding all times of the year. Even with modern transportation, it is still not easy to get to these villages of the Aravis; that's part of the appeal of the place for those who enjoy the splendors of an outdoor holiday today. Imagine, even more, how difficult it was to come and go from such a place five hundred years ago.

The peaks in the region range from 6,800 to 10,700 feet, and for three seasons of each year these altitudes were Faber's workplace. It was a boy's job to help tend his father's flock, a responsibility that tends to be boring ninety-nine hours out of a hundred and terrifying for the one remaining. To lose sight of a sheep on a lazy summer afternoon is to imagine your father's wrath when you return home. Sheep also make for company that lulls the senses, especially for a sensitive boy with an eidetic memory. Peter spent long hours each day on ridges and in meadows with those sheep. He watched seasons change dramatically, with snows melting into spring torrents, warm sun bringing to life brilliant green blankets of grass and sudden carpets of blue flowers.

We know from the memoir he wrote that Peter didn't treasure the beauty, serenity, and wildlife of his childhood, at least not enough to record memories of it. He instead seems to have begun seeking out people—anyone to talk with. Soldiers returning from wars. Friars preaching rules of life and ways of repentance. Heretics doing the same—it was often difficult to tell the difference. Poets, often former friars, with bawdy songs. Peter soon knew them, just as he could recite every word of the catechism back to his mother by the time he was five.

His early life was full of these peaks and valleys, odd characters and hiding heretics, for the mountains were known to shelter those living outside the Catholic Church. People knew that landslides and avalanches were killers, that the mountains were not a safe place to be. Many associated fear with the mountains: "Dragons and ogres prowled their summits. They rudely got in the way of travel to important places, like Rome. They were God's punishment for man's sinfulness."[10] In the Savoy Prealps, one lived among a mix of the bucolic and the backward, the hidden and the subversive.

There is great beauty in this land that is shared today by France, Switzerland, and Italy. It is where one finds towns and communes with names like Chambéry, Chamonix ("Chamouni" in the poems of the English Romantic poets), Valloire, Moûtiers (formerly Tarentaise), La Motte-Servolex, and Valmeinier. These are remote places with tiny populations, numbering in the hundreds, nestled into soaring mountains. Small rivers pour into Lake Annecy, where Faber swam as a boy. Northwest of the port cities of Nice and Genoa, north of Monaco, and west of Turin, these were the feudal lands of the House of Savoy, one of the oldest and most respected of the royal families of Europe.

The Holy Roman Emperor Sigismund of Luxemburg made the Savoy an independent duchy in 1416, ruled by its own duke, removing for a while the ability of French, Spanish, and Italian princes to fight over it. Always a strategic entry point from France into Italy (over the mountains), the Duchy of Savoy would remain a place of small towns and an agricultural economy, but it became of military importance throughout the interminable wars over control of northern Italy between the kingdoms of Spain and France. In Faber's time, Savoy knights became Savoy kings who ruled that territory, and beyond, all the way to the unification of Italy in 1861, when popes and their papal land grabs came to an official end and the sovereign state of tiny Vatican City was created. That son of Savoy was Victor Emmanuel II, king of Italy in 1861, the first king in twelve centuries. His people dubbed him *Padre della Patria*, "father of the fatherland." Then, on maps the Savoy dissolved into the Kingdom of Sardinia, linked geographically to the rest of Italy: Lombardy-Venetia, Tuscany, the Papal States, and the Two Sicilies.

But in Faber's childhood, the Savoy was mostly peaceful. While tending those sheep, Peter experienced the natural beauty that one can still see in the paintings of Henri Matisse and Ferdinand Hodler. Hodler's landscape *Rising Mist over the Savoy Alps* (1917), dreamy and fierce, with the sun rising over wet, purple-valleyed cliffs, communicates those peaceful places well. So do some lines from Percy Bysshe Shelley:

Far, far above, piercing the infinite sky,
Mont Blanc appears,—still, snowy, and serene—
Its subject mountains their unearthly forms
Pile around it, ice and rock; broad vales between
Of frozen floods, unfathomable deeps,
Blue as the overhanging heaven, that spread
And wind among the accumulated steeps.
    —from Mont Blanc: Lines written in the Vale of Chamouni, 60–66

But childhood wasn't precious back then. Boys were supposed to be men, and girls, women. We see this in artistic renderings of infants with muscles and boys with adult faces. In both work and play children mixed with adults. There was little protection in childhood. Parents routinely saw children die in infancy. The writer Michel de Montaigne, who was just a generation younger than Faber, remarked in an essay that he lost "two or three children" during their infancy—a terrible experience by any standards, but it demonstrates the stoicism that was typical amid common infant mortality.

A mountain hamlet was a safe place to be, even if the mountains themselves weren't always, but no one was immune from the violence of those days. Criminals were punished severely. It was common to happen upon a man in the stocks or being strangled, hanged, or even quartered according to the law—these were common sentences for crimes of robbery and murder. Heretics were even more severely dealt with, and friars were often hounding them, even into Faber's mountains. One man's place of refuge was another's place of bait. Even religious orders—monks in monasteries—were known to be violent; brawls and murders were not uncommon between religious who were disputing some detail of their life together.[11]

Meanwhile, stories circulated of men and women from a time not so distant: stories of exemplary figures of what Christians call *sanctus*, "holy ones," or saints. Saints were human beings who had died and had unquestionably gone to heaven. From their holy vantage point, the saints were able to champion the lives and causes of those who were left on the earth. To saints, men and women fervently prayed.

By the end of his first decade, Faber had nothing to complain about, but life in a hamlet wasn't going to satisfy him. The dumb animal stares, the stubborn silliness of a flock, were his primary occupations until he was old enough to articulate that this was not what his heart desired.

"What do you want, then, if not this?" his father would say, exasperation showing.

"I don't know," Peter replied at first.

He was still a boy, and he wouldn't know what he really wanted until later when one of his roommates at the University of Paris began to speak—it seemed—to his soul. But that's to jump ahead in the story. For now, all Peter knew was that he wanted to go to school.

## Early Schooling

Would anyone be surprised if a curious boy with intellectual gifts wanted something more beyond tending sheep? Many among his extended family and neighbors surely faulted Peter for this desire. What an ingrate, they probably said. He doesn't know how good he has it!

One of Peter's uncles—his father's brother—was then prior of the Carthusian charterhouse in nearby Le Reposoir. The word *reposoir* means "resting place," and the town got its name from Carthusian monks in 1151 who were looking for farmland and a quiet place to pray. The presence of Father Mamert Faber close by shows that religious life might have run in the family. Also, Peter's knowledge of his uncle the friar must have made it more disappointing and confusing to him when his parents were less than enthusiastic about his pleading. Could it be that Peter's father was resentful of his brother, the prior, and the leisure afforded him for prayer and study? Such tensions have existed in families for centuries, particularly when elder brothers have responsibilities that younger ones do not. A hagiographer once wrote, "Peter found in Dom Favre a wise counselor from whom he received constant guidance and advice," but there is little evidence for this.[12] As in most matters of searching for Peter Faber, silence is one of the most interesting pieces of evidence. Peter does not mention his uncle. The tradition says that Dom Mamert watched over his nephew, but it may be just as likely that Faber's parents kept him as far from the boy as possible.

By the time Peter was ten, Louis and Marie chose to listen to their son, recognizing that his qualities seemed to set him apart from the other members of the family. So they sent him to school six miles away from Le Villaret, in Thônes. Today the town of Thônes is in France, about thirty-five miles south of Geneva, Switzerland. Geneva sits at the extreme western tip of Switzerland and is almost as close geographically to Milan as it is to Zurich.

In 1516, Thônes was part of the diocese of Geneva, a place that Faber poignantly recalls—when the fledgling Reformation made such terms a necessary form of currency—as "very Catholic." Geneva was part of the Duchy of Savoy until 1526, when the city sought to realign with the Swiss Confederation, as feelings of Swiss independence and pride were on a dramatic rise. This was also brought on, and then exacerbated by, Protestant influence in the region. The Catholic bishop of Geneva fled the city, and the radical Protestant reformer Ulrich Zwingli, of Zurich, flooded in along with his overenthusiastic followers. This was not the calm and neutrality that the Swiss are known for today.

It was in Thônes where Faber quickly learned how to read and write. Even if later accounts of his childhood preaching are to be believed, the boy was still illiterate before going off to school. After Thônes he moved a few more miles away to another school, this time in La Roche-sur-Foron, in the Auvergne-Rhone Alps, very near to the town where his parents had baptized him and near the medieval Château d'Annecy, once home to the Counts of Geneva. At the new school, his master was Pierre Velliard, a Swiss priest, whom Peter remembered as saintly, perhaps because everything related to school was holy in his eyes. "All the poets and authors he read with us seemed to be like gospels," Faber recounts in his *Memoriale*, the memoir of his experiences. At La Roche-sur-Foron, Faber studied until the age of nineteen, by which time he was reading and responding to one of the classic theological and philosophical texts of the age: the Fourth Book of Peter Lombard's *Sentences*. For the rest of his life, Peter would regard education as a gift that saved him from a life of meaninglessness and dissolution.

There are no praises of bucolic scenery and contemporary idylls in Faber's writings. One even wonders whether he was familiar with earlier writings of the saints, including the "Canticle of the Creatures" by Francis of Assisi, that praise the created world. Such reflections were rare in Francis's time and even rarer in Faber's day. Faber probably read in school, however, the great Italian poet Petrarch, who rhapsodized on the tranquility the soul experienced in ancient forests and how the warmth of the sun or a cool breeze felt like love between lovers. But Petrarch was the exception, and that was literature.

With the broader perspective that formal education gave him, Faber began to speak of his childhood sins as if they were very great, when they were probably mild by any modern standard. "I could have become like Sodom and Gomorrah!" he once exclaimed in his journal, later in life, and surely that's how he felt. It was common for a Christian man well schooled in faith to view his flesh as his most real enemy. This is the language, for example, of the letters of St. Paul. "The wisdom of the flesh is an enemy to God," Paul says. And, "For we know that the law is spiritual; but I am carnal, sold under sin."[13] These teachings are still in Christian Scripture today, of course; however, they no longer carry the same literal sense they once did. We don't read St. Paul in his letter to the Romans as Faber's generation did: "Unhappy man that I am, who shall deliver me from the body of this death?"[14] Paul meant it, literally; he believed that death was preferable to life. Many among the devout prayed that God would permit them to die—and preferably as martyrs. Faber felt similar things, and deeply, and he also had the flair of a dramatist. But the love for learning that Faber knew was also a grace of God in his life. Learning was sacramental for him. As Faber writes concerning books on study, "[They] willed to draw me away from my flesh and from my nature."[15]

## Going Home and Leaving Home

Two years after going away to school, Faber was home for summer holidays one day, again shepherding in the hills for his father. He was overcome with emotion and love for God and learning, and he made a promise of lifelong chastity to demonstrate this devotion. He whispered it quietly to himself and God. Then, having privately marked himself for religious life, Peter began to see himself in the psalms of David, lamenting with phrases lifted from the lines of that shepherd-turned-king: "O mercy of God, you walked at my side and longed for me! Ah, Lord, why did I not recognize you clearly from that time on? O Holy Spirit, why . . . was I not able to separate myself from all things so as to seek you?"[16] These words were originally written by a middle-aged King David who wished he had spent the days of his youth differently: "He asked you for life; you gave it to him—length of days forever and ever" (Ps. 21:4). Faber, too, was vowing to do differently with his life going forward, but unlike David, he was doing so from his relative youth.

Faber spent the following nine years between school and occasional holidays at home. By the time he was ready to leave La Roche, at nineteen, another soon-to-be prominent reformer, John Calvin, only three years younger than Faber, was living nearby in the diocese of Geneva, intent on becoming a priest, studying philosophy and law. This is what Peter wanted, as well: to continue his education at one of the great universities. His next step would be the adventure of traveling to Paris, to figure out more of who he was. Faber prepared to leave for university, saying that it was "through the inclination [to study that] our Lord took me away from my country." There is no sense that he was sad about it but rather that he saw the opportunity as a great blessing.

# 2

# Meanwhile in Germany

*So wie das Geld im Kasten klingt, die Seele aus dem Fegfeuer springt.*
*As soon as the gold in the box rings, the rescued soul to heaven springs.*
—John Tetzel

## 1513—1516

History sometimes turns on small events. Most often we're unaware of them, alive, as we are, in the middle of what's happening. One of these "small" events in Peter Faber's life took place when he was not yet seven years old.

Imagine a quiet morning in early 1513 when the twenty-two-year-old Albert of Brandenburg, youngest son of John Cicero, elector of Brandenburg, fourth of the House of Hohenzollern, decided over morning coffee to enter the Catholic Church for his profession. Albert's father was dead, and Albert's older brother had already inherited his father's electorship, as well as the House of Hohenzollern. So, Albert needed his own way to advance in the world. The church offered many opportunities to someone of his lineage and background. Brandenburg family influence gave Albert at least enough currency to effortlessly become archbishop of Magdeburg—at only twenty-three!

A year later, Albert's ambition expanded further. He wanted to be primate of all Germany, which was then the most influential state of the Holy Roman Empire, by becoming the archbishop-elector of Mainz. Then he would truly be a "Prince of the Church." We use that term today to refer to cardinals, but in Albert's day a prince of the church was one whose authority in the religious realm was equivalent to that of royalty. The privileges of such a prince—in land, wealth, authority, influence—were tremendous.

Albert's cardinal's hat could only come from Pope Leo X, and Leo gave it to him easily. But it wasn't free. Albert had to pay for that hat and pallium to the tune of twenty-five thousand gold ducats. This is how it often worked—and it was for this reason, needing to raise some serious funds, that Albert, again with Leo X's blessing, turned to a salesman by the name of John Tetzel to offer indulgences to the faithful. An indulgence was a promise for the forgiveness of sins that was, for a time, obtained by anyone with money to purchase it. Indulgence slips were among the first texts printed on Gutenberg's presses. They usually even carried expiration dates, not unlike a container of milk today. Tetzel would make sales of promissory notes to earn back the cash Albert needed, helping him repay his loan for the cardinal's hat. It was Tetzel's remarkable salesmanship and success that attracted the attention of a young Augustinian friar by the name of Martin Luther.

If only Albert had decided to go into law!

Luther's abhorrence of the sale of indulgences would become just one piece of his objection to medieval Catholic spiritual theology. You cannot buy bits of forgiveness, let alone obtain forgiveness at the hand of a priest, Luther would soon say. He watched John Tetzel with growing fury.

Luther had good reason for that anger and, soon, for his protests. Simony—the purchase of church positions and spiritual favors—was rife in the church at every level. Religious illiteracy and insincerity among the clergy were commonplace. Immorality among church leaders, often of an openly sexual nature, was also too common. But the friar's views on how a Christian may come to know and understand God put him out of step with a long line of Catholic tradition. At the Diet of Worms, when Faber was a teenager, Luther fired back at those accusing him of heresy: "Unless I am convinced by the testimony of Scripture or evident reason . . . I am bound to the Scriptures which I have adduced and my conscience is captive to the Word of God."[17]

The sale of indulgences would eventually lead Luther to want to overturn the entire medieval Catholic approach to sanctification. His approach suggested that spiritual growth is a direct result of hard work. The asceticism, prayer, Scripture reading, and contemplation of monks in monasteries and mystics in cells are unnecessary for—and perhaps even hinder, Luther provocatively claimed—an intimate understanding of God. The extravagance of simony and Luther's exaggerations fueled the Reformation, and a division between "faith" and "works" was off to the races. On this subject, Protestants and Catholics still misinterpret each other five hundred years later. This is how one Protestant historian recently explained Luther's approach inaugurated so long ago:

> This is the genius of Reformation spirituality. It assumes that the simplest believer leaps to the top of the spirituality ladder simply by realistic faith in Jesus Christ. Consistent Protestants start every day at the top of the ladder, receiving by faith what only God can give and what cannot be achieved by human efforts: assurance of salvation, and the guiding presence of the Holy Spirit. They may slip down a few rungs during the course of the day, but the way up again is not by climbing. It is by the vault of faith.[18]

When the Reformation first happened, Faber was still in school, only dreaming of university. But in years soon to come, he would be grieved by this Protestant "genius," and he'd want those inspired by Luther to see all that they were missing by leaving the Catholic sacraments behind. When Faber saw what was happening, he wanted the reformers to come back into the fold, for their sakes and for his.

# 3

# Walking to Paris

*Wonder is the desire of knowledge.*
—St. Thomas Aquinas

## Summer 1525

Peter Faber must have prepared mightily for the journey he undertook in September 1525. He was accepted and ready to enroll at the University of Paris—but first he had to get himself there.

Could he have known what turmoil the world was in at the time? The French crown had been decisively defeated on February 24 in Pavia, Lombardy, in the northern part of the Italian Peninsula. The defeat was the turning point in what was called the Four Years' War or the Italian Wars, pitting France and the Republic of Venice against England, the Papal States, and those loyal to the Holy Roman Emperor. This was the first of the era's many religiously inspired conflicts, brought on by the Protestant rebellion taking place throughout Europe. Royal players in this chess match-turned-war were at the height of their young powers: King Henry VIII of England was thirty-three; King Francis I of France was thirty; and Holy Roman Emperor Charles V was just twenty-five—all young men wanting to make names for themselves.

Henry VIII had invaded France two years earlier. Francis I had just marched through Milan, installing his own governor there. But at the Battle of Pavia, Francis was roundly defeated, watching as most of his nobles died on the battlefield and later taken captive himself. Francis would be held by Charles V in a citadel in Spain and forced the following January to sign the Treaty of Madrid, renouncing all of France's claims to the lands of Italy, Flanders, and even Burgundy. This is what was happening back and forth across the Alps as Faber set out to go to university to study.

There was a new kind of cynicism about people in power that was becoming more common. Any innocence that had existed in people's imaginations about kings and queens, princes and rulers, even cardinals and bishops in the Catholic Church was quickly vanishing. The Italian humanist and diplomat Niccolò Machiavelli's shock-packed little book *The Prince* (1513) had much to do with this. Picking up where Dante Alighieri had left off two centuries earlier with his treatise *De Monarchia*, Machiavelli exposed how the powerful think and the cunning approaches they use to achieve power, for all to see. Machiavelli offered bits of sage advice, giving birth to modern political science in the process:

> A lion cannot protect himself from traps, and a fox cannot defend himself from a pack of wolves. One must therefore be like a fox recognizing traps, and like a lion scaring away wolves.
>
> One who uses the skills of a fox to his advantage is always the most successful.
>
> A wise ruler should not keep to his word if it becomes a disadvantage for him to do so. . . . If everyone was naturally good, this rule wouldn't be necessary.
>
> A good deceiver will always find one willing to be deceived.[19]

Never mind world events and world leaders: there were also more mundane, everyday worries to consider. Traveling in the company of others, Faber would have been fearful of what could happen to him alone on the road in such remote places. Simply the physiology of a long journey in the sixteenth century would instruct those upon it in ways a twenty-first-century traveler can hardly imagine. Whether by foot, steed, or ship, one lumbered slowly and vulnerably along the way. The time the journey took was essential to the experience of what journeying meant and its potential dangers.

This was no longer the old Roman Empire, with its protections and safeties for citizens, and roads were not even "roads" much of the time; they were mountain passes and valleys, cart paths and gravel roads that often washed away in springtime floods, filled with discreet places where robbers and bandits took shelter. Travel was dangerous along medieval highways and byways, let alone more remote paths and passes. Many of those who lingered there were men not welcome in cities and towns—thieves and bullies looking for easy victims traveling without weapons, on their own, usually with money or valuables. This short passage from a guide for pilgrims written originally in France in the twelfth century explains a great deal that held true for centuries. It advises caution with regard to crossing rivers and avoiding bad men:

> At a place called Lorca . . . runs a river called the Salty Brook. Be careful not to let it touch your lips or allow your horse to drink there, for this river is deadly! On its bank, while we were going to Santiago, we met two men of Navarre sitting sharpening their knives; they are in the habit of skinning the mounts of pilgrims who drink that water and die. When questioned by us, these liars said that it was safe to drink. We therefore watered our horses, and immediately two of them died, which these people skinned on the spot.[20]

A search for Peter Faber leads through these places throughout his life, beginning with his journey to Paris. And from the time he set off on that journey, Faber would spend an extraordinary number of his days traveling by foot and by mount all across Europe.

The bedrock of the alpine mountain passes is limestone, and the region was then nearly covered in forest. Ancient volcanoes had cut lakes into densely wooded gorges. There are moments when the face of some of the mountains falls several hundred yards into summit ridges. Troops that were Spanish, French, and German had marched in these valleys and across these gorges but never to the point of making roads that could be maintained or defended.

As Faber and his companions—we don't know who they were—walked, they were at times very near the Via Francigena (literally, "The Road from France"), an ancient passageway that originated in the city of Rome and traveled all the way to the North Sea. This is the road that established cities such as Vercelli, Lausanne, Reims, and Lyon; provided entries to the lush vineyards of Champagne and Arras; and traveled all the way to Calais. Faber surely knew of others—perhaps even family or friends—who had traveled this way; for four centuries, Paris and the Paris Basin had become "unusually economically active," according to one historian of that period. Such activity, the historian points out, provides "a basic context for the growth of the Paris schools and, later, university (for there was no point attracting students if there was no infrastructure to feed them)."[21]

Three centuries earlier every city in northern France had begun to build a soaring Gothic cathedral, availing themselves of some of that infrastructure, as well as natural resources, and the resources of people (to do the work) who were being attracted to the cities at an increasing rate.

Faber and his cohort were probably often traveling off-path, on a similar trajectory but to the west of the Via Francigena. They would have walked through Dijon, crossing paths with pilgrims on the old, medieval route that began near Trier to the north and continued directly southward to Arles, where they took a right turn toward the Atlantic, across northern Spain, to Santiago de Compostela. Days later, Faber would have passed near Troyes, closer to Paris. All total, this journey must have taken several weeks.

# 4

## Interlude: "I had a great longing to yield to Christ in my heart's center."

Toward the end of his short life, Peter Faber wrote a brief spiritual memoir that was found in the middle of the nineteenth century, almost by accident. This book—which we've alluded to a few times already—is titled *Memoriale*, a Latin word that means "memorial" or "memories," and it had been lost to history for three hundred years. Only in the middle of the nineteenth century was it found and published, too quietly, by members of the Society of Jesus. It is a spiritual classic that is still almost unknown to most Christians.

When we read *Memoriale*, which was written truly (and deliberately) without literary grace, we are eavesdropping on a personal, two-sided conversation. There is no monologue because Faber, unsurprisingly, isn't trying to instruct or impress anyone. There also is not the loneliness that often accompanies private journaling. What we find instead is a constant seeking and gleaning of spiritual presence. We see Faber attempting to discern and apply the presence of God to the progression of his soul. Faber wrote it for the benefit of other Jesuits. It is not a self-portrait, something Faber would never have considered creating. What happens in *Memoriale* is commonly associated with methods of Ignatian discernment—that is, a way of discernment described in writings of Ignatius of Loyola and developed in retreatants through his Spiritual Exercises.

It seems unusual that Faber began this style of introspective writing only four years before he died because he knew (all the early Jesuits knew) that Ignatius recorded every day what was happening in his soul. One wonders if Faber did the same over the years, since first learning of Iñigo's practice at the

University of Paris, but most of those reflections have been lost. Could this be why, at the start of *Memoriale*, Faber offers a brief summary of his life story? If so, that's a terrible shame, but history is littered with sources that have been lost . . . This is what we *do* have.

Peter clearly knew God in intimate terms. He speaks of a "hidden dwelling" inside of him where God, and no one else, is known.

This first short passage is from *Memoriale* 68 (editors have numbered the book's sections to make referring to them universal). More than any other, this selection lies at the center of Faber's spirituality. It is as good a place to begin as any, as it reflects Peter's desire from childhood, a desire that was then fulfilled and deepened at every stage in his life: soon after he met Ignatius in Paris and then more so once he had discovered what Iñigo revealed to him through the Spiritual Exercises.

Imagine the scene. Perhaps you have had a similar experience. Peter is at Mass (in his case, he is celebrating at Mass) when he feels powerfully moved by God. Deep emotion during Mass is the experience of many people, and Peter was no exception.

The day was August 7, 1542—seventeen years later than where we left off in the mostly chronological account of his life in this book. It was the feast of St. Dominic—not the Dominic who founded the Dominican Order but rather St. Dominic the Carthusian. From that moment, Peter records, "I had a great longing."

> Would that my whole inner being, especially my heart, were so yielding to Christ coming in as to open up and leave to him the place in my heart's center.

He seems to be thinking not just spiritually but also physiologically. He is imagining opening himself up and yielding his heart to Christ fully. This couldn't help but influence the everyday decisions he would make and where his life would take him.

# 5

# Bright Lights, Big University

*Faber could discern God's voice in his desires. One goes nowhere without desire and that is why we need to offer our own desires to the Lord.*[22]
—Pope Francis

### October 1525–1529

The smell nearly knocked him off his feet as he descended from the carriage in the Latin Quarter, home to the University of Paris and its thousands of students. What was causing that stench? The Parisian sanitation specialty, *tout à la rue*, or "all in the street," was out in full force. And there it was, too, affronting Faber's nose, his eyes, his feet! He didn't really want to know that eventually all those unpleasant things ended up in the River Seine. Faber simply put a sleeve over his nose as he picked up the bags holding everything he owned.

He had just walked the 350 miles from his home in the Savoy to Paris, and it had been no pilgrimage. Stepping off the carriage late that afternoon in September 1525, Peter surely felt a sense of both exhilaration and terror. The boulevards of Paris were a long way from the Alps he'd always called home. Some people find the nine-thousand-foot peak of Pointe Percée daunting, but he knew it well. The scope of Paris was another thing entirely. At nineteen, already a man by most standards of the day, he knew that his life hadn't even yet begun. He hadn't really done anything, not yet.

Who was he? He wouldn't know the answer for at least five more years. But finally, he was where he wanted to be: Paris.

Faber did know a few things for certain. For one, he desperately didn't want to be a shepherd any longer. He'd tended enough sheep and milked enough

23

cows to last a lifetime. The sounds he knew were animal and human: babies crying, horses baying, pigs snorting, and geese honking. He knew the domestic and the rural. To a boy with an active imagination, the occasional rumbling past of ox-driven carts or a village smith clanging his irons wasn't enough to satisfy his senses. He also knew that he wanted to study and learn. And he had already dedicated his life to God. What would that mean for him?

There had for centuries been three classes of men (women were class bound in different ways), and each man was destined to pursue one of them: soldiers or knights, monks and clerics, or the working class. Faber's immediate family was of the last, but he had relatives from the religious class: monks and priests. The praying class was also the only one that was expected—and permitted—to read and study. Divisions between those who are brawny and those who are brainy are nothing new; they existed then, too. The brawny fighting men, who went out to defend everyone when wars broke out, disdained the "weaker" ones who didn't. And reading men often looked upon those who didn't read as "ignorant of God as beasts, or cruel in their use of arms and guilty of crime," as an earlier monastic Frenchman once put it.[23]

Peter Faber loved books and lived in a time when those who were hungry for ideas and the written word suddenly had access to both. One no longer had to become a monk to be around books. That said, he would probably end up in a monastery anyhow. He'd even taken that private vow of celibacy, years earlier, just as he reached the age of accountability. He wanted to become a priest, maybe more.

Stepping into the streets of Paris for the first time, he noticed the lights. Streetlamps, lit by thousands of candles on either side of the Seine, caused the cathedrals, shops, and residence windows to shine in the hour just after sunset. Dark, moonless nights had formed Faber, but now they were part of his past. Blinkered by the city, simultaneously intrigued by and afraid of its people, noises, and filth, Peter was filled with curiosity. He was going to throw himself into university life and the experiences of Paris as he began to explore Europe's largest city.

He walked around the City of Lights and took in the points and arches of Gothic architecture. Nighttime was a special time of wonderment—all he'd known before arriving in Paris was the country and mountain night sky. When clear, it dazzled; when overcast, a person might fall into a ditch or ravine on a simple walk home. In the city, though, Faber was surrounded by new lights: candle lanterns lit, hanging, up and down city streets by Parisian ordinance, and torchbearers-for-hire strolling along the banks of the Seine. He passed mendicants in gray and black robes, begging alms, and some of the desperately poor—neither of whom he'd encountered much up until that point.

There was more to be discovered. Notre-Dame and Sainte-Chapelle held heavenly treasures. Peter's fellow students would soon be freely quoting, revering, and imitating poets like Petrarch and satirists like Boccaccio. Book publishing was flourishing, as the city's literati vied with Venice to dominate the new industry of print. All the friends he would soon have, who shared the interests he had long nourished! Peter had always made friends easily, and now the Latin Quarter and its sixty colleges were filled with possibilities.

## University Life

In Paris, Faber's mind began to receive the stimulation it had craved. A new humanism had started to take root in the Collège Sainte-Barbe in the decades before Peter's arrival, and the variety of learning deeply fed the young man—who already thought of learning and study as his salvation. Just as students at Harvard, Yale, or Stanford today might realize that they are sitting in class beside future Nobel winners and chairmen of the Federal Reserve, so did students of the University of Paris in the time of Faber realize that they were likely seated beside a future cardinal, king, doctor of the church, or pope.

Danes, Swedes, Germans, and Scots each had their own colleges where they willingly segregated. They lived among one another, though, desiring to speak a similar language, and took meals together. The English, for instance, were all over Paris, most of them Catholics living in exile. In 1525—several years before King Henry VIII was excommunicated by the pope and declared himself Supreme Head of the Church of England—England was already unfriendly to Catholics, and many of them sent their sons to Paris to study. Later it would become treasonous, not just dangerous, to be Catholic in England. In this way, the early decades of the sixteenth century at the University of Paris were an "open" time, welcoming exiles and foreigners and embracing a diverse student body.[24] Students with common studies, such as the visual arts, formed social groups as well. To be outside of one of these special groupings of men was to take part in a Mediterranean, more European, experience in Paris. Portuguese and Spaniards dominated the Collège Sainte-Barbe.

## Growing Religious Tensions

Before he arrived, Faber probably knew very little about the Sorbonne, Paris's theological college, except what most everyone knew: humanists like Erasmus of Rotterdam were unwelcome, and there was little tolerance for reformers. Tradition was upheld in Paris; innovation was frowned upon.

One former university rector had held an inquest seventy-five years earlier to retry Joan of Arc, the burned-at-the-stake heroine of France. And within a few years of Luther's Ninety-Five Theses, the Sorbonne faculty condemned the reformer's work. Despite all of this, Faber was a student in Paris at a turning point when new ideas were increasingly met with openness, even when not from those in authority. A century later, Paris would become a progressive city compared to a place like Rome, where Galileo was investigated, and nearly convicted, by the new branch of Inquisition established in 1542, named "Roman" for the city of its nexus. Unlike the Spanish Inquisition, which was aimed mostly at rooting out "secret" Jews and Muslims in the nervous Christian population of late-medieval Spain, the Roman Inquisition was the next century's tool of the pope in response to the bungled handling of Luther's complaints and protests.[25]

Lutherans and Protestants may have been kept away from Paris, but their publications could not be controlled. Printing centers surrounded the city like a besieging army. Technically, Protestant books—the era's contraband—were illegal to possess, but students have been similar in every era and place, and they found ways to rebel and obtain them from Mainz, Antwerp, and Basel.

The Sorbonne was the first college of the University of Paris, founded in the thirteenth century by Robert de Sorbon, the first figure to begin to transform the master-pupil relationship into a more formal college setting. Students would come to Paris and gather around charismatic figures like Peter Abelard, an earlier era's famous master. In Abelard's thirteenth century, the university system was not a university at all but a loose network of masters with pupils: "The student followed lectures given by that master, and when his studies were completed, he asked the master to present him to obtain the degree."[26] Masters didn't house or feed any of their students until Robert de Sorbon started the first of these "pedagogies," as universities were sometimes called. The model he relied on most was the medieval monastic system. Just like at a monastery, parents could consider their child taken care of, body and mind, by leaving him safeguarded with Master Sorbon at the Sorbonne, for example. Orthodoxy was to be protected and upheld. Also, to reside and study with a master, or at a college, was to commit oneself fully to the work. At the Sorbonne, that work was preaching and teaching within the church, and so the statutes for that college read, "Those who reside in the house, shall within a short space of time prepare and dispose themselves to make progress in public sermons throughout the parishes and in disputations and lectures in the schools."[27] But this wasn't Faber's calling.

Outside Paris, a growing riot was of course taking place in the Catholic Church, instigated by those who were calling themselves Protestants. The word *Protestant* stems from words in both German and English that mean "protest"—the Protestants were protesting the unanimity of the Catholic Church. One of these, an intellectual colleague of Martin Luther in Geneva named John Calvin, was even studying philosophy in one of Paris's colleges in the same first year as Faber. But the University of Paris wanted nothing to do with the Protestants and their protests. Theologically speaking, theirs was a place for Scholastic scholarship and precision. The great Thomas Aquinas, the "Angelic Doctor," was still in command 250 years after his death.

Faber enrolled at the Collège Sainte-Barbe, just a few generations young, where the new humanism was flourishing like cherry blossoms in a Parisian spring. It was flourishing so much, in fact, that France's King Francis I would, a few years later, found the new Collège de France across the street from the Sorbonne as a purely humanist institution, quite apart from the training of men for careers in the Catholic Church.

# 6

# Meanwhile in Spain

*[In Spanish Catholicism], those who ignored death would pay a high price when their time came. . . . Living through death in one's mind involved nothing less than contemplating the putrefaction of one's flesh and pondering the ultimate futility of all carnal pursuits.*[28]
—Carlos M. N. Eire

## 1521–1529

At the western end of the European continent, not far from France and Germany, yet very far away, in Spain, Catholics thought themselves the saviors of the faith. There, this Protestantism was a new and apostate religion. Little did Faber know when he arrived in Paris how his life would be changed by two men from this part of the world. One was Faber's exact contemporary; the other was nearly old enough to be his father.

In Spain in the early sixteenth century, Catholics felt that it was their job to buttress the church while it was under assault. They knew about assaults on Christian faith, having thrown off only a generation earlier the last of the Muslim rulers—who'd first crossed the Straits of Gibraltar from Morocco in 711 and ruled the Iberian Peninsula for eight centuries.

One of the most famous painters in Spain at that time was the Dutchman Hieronymus Bosch, and the popularity of his work in staunchly traditional Catholic Spain speaks volumes. This painter's macabre visions of hell were copied all over the continent. Giorgio Vasari, renowned critic and Bosch's contemporary, praised Bosch's works while referring to them as "fantastic and wanton." Bosch's art told stories of what ordinary people most dreaded: figures in the woods, demons at nighttime, and fury in the depths of the human soul. He was a hit in Spain. Reproductions of his work proliferated.

Bosch's famous triptych, *The Garden of Earthly Delights*, depicts his view of human history from beginning to end. It shows Adam and Eve in the Garden of Eden in the first panel on the left, followed by joyful, cavorting people on the middle panel, and then a dark, dismal, hellish depiction of the Last Judgment on the right. Another painting by this apocalyptic artist, representative of his full body of work, is *The Last Judgment*. It shows people in agony in all sorts of ways, the sort of agony that the apocalypse depicts as happening to human beings by God's hand but violence that people of Bosch's century knew from the human hand.

The intensity of Bosch's paintings seemed to demand a viewing, and people seemed to intuitively understand that these images of tortures, weeping, demons, witches, skeletons, and people doing the most awful things depicted what lurks inside each person. As Sister Wendy Beckett put it in *The Story of Painting*: "The sinister and monstrous things that he brought forth are the hidden creatures of our inward self-love: he externalizes the ugliness within, and so his misshapen demons have an effect beyond curiosity." It is difficult to take your eyes off Bosch's creations; they seem to pessimistically foretell how the rest of the century would go.

The birthplace of ardent mystics and fierce loyalists to the Roman Catholic Church, Spain was also the country that, a generation before Faber's, had expelled, executed, or enslaved its Jewish and Muslim citizens. Its rulers then set out to conquer and enslave faraway lands in the Americas in the name of Christian faith and piety. "War against the infidels" was the Spanish motto under King Ferdinand and Queen Isabella, which, as one of the great historians of the twentieth century put it, "contained both the grandeur and the misery of the Spanish people."[29]

## Iñigo López de Loyola

A roster of famous saints was born into this sixteenth-century environment of Catholic fervor in Spain. One immediately thinks of Teresa of Ávila (1515–1582) and John of the Cross (1542–1591), but Spanish Catholicism also produced three of the most important Jesuits in history. Each is a principal character in our story, chief among them Iñigo López de Loyola.

Around the time that Hieronymous Bosch was painting *The Garden of Earthly Delights*, there was every indication that Iñigo would become a man of power, fame, and influence in the new world, which had long ago replaced its garden with more earthly preoccupations. Such qualities were the only ones that men imagined could make one successful. Iñigo was a soldier, but not an ordinary one, for he was also suave and handsome, "his cape slinging open to reveal his tight-fitting hose and boots; a sword and dagger at his waist," as one of his many biographers puts it.[30] Eventually, Iñigo came to serve Charles V, the Holy Roman Emperor, grandson of Ferdinand II. Charles V was, like Iñigo, a worldly man, a man of many countries, languages, and allegiances. He was said to have quipped, "I speak Spanish to God, Italian to women, French to men, and German to my horse." Charles V spent most of the 1520s fighting the Ottoman Turks on one side of his empire and the French on the other.

The turning point in Iñigo's life came in May 1521. He was inside the fortress in Pamplona, Spain, which was under siege by the French. Charles V was in Worms (today's Germany) presiding over an imperial assembly where young Martin Luther was being asked to account for his challenges to the authority of the Catholic Church. As emperor, Charles was responsible for defending the church's honor, and as a devout Catholic, he took this responsibility seriously enough to be present in Worms. He was also acutely conscious of papal power to the south, and it was in his interest that the pope's power not be destabilized.

Luther's testimony at the Diet of Worms is quite famous. He didn't exactly say, as tradition goes, "Here I stand; I can do no other!" At least there is no direct testimony to that effect. But he did say, "Unless I am convinced by the testimony of the Scriptures or by clear reason (for I do not trust either in the pope or in councils alone, since it is well known that they have often erred and contradicted themselves), I am bound by the Scriptures I have quoted and my conscience is captive to the Word of God. I cannot and will not recant anything, since it is neither safe nor right to go against conscience. May God help me."[31] Even so, Charles V let Luther go rather than execute him as the heretic he was declared to be, especially since Charles's Edict of Worms, issued on May 26, forcefully stated: "We forbid anyone from this time forward to dare, either by words or by deeds, to receive, defend, sustain, or favor the said Martin Luther. On the contrary, we want him to be apprehended and punished as a notorious heretic, as he deserves, to be brought personally before us, or to be securely guarded until those who have captured him inform us, whereupon we will order the appropriate manner of proceeding against the said Luther. Those who will help in his capture will be rewarded generously for their good work."

One didn't become emperor without knowing how to connive. Charles calculated that allowing Luther to escape Worms with his freedom and life was the course of action that would lead to the least amount of trouble throughout the empire.

Back in Pamplona, thirty-year-old Iñigo and other local subjects of the emperor knew of upstart Protestants, and they'd heard of Luther the heretic, but they were gathered to defend a citadel. For more than a decade, Iñigo had strutted around Spain with cape, sword, and dagger, a military enthusiast with a hot head and too much testosterone. Once, at about the age of twenty, he'd encountered a Moor who spoke against the divinity of Christ. Iñigo challenged the man to a duel and killed him. In Pamplona, on that May afternoon in 1521 that was the turning point of his life, as a participant in what historians today call the Hapsburg-Valois Wars (1494–1559), he was defending the citadel of Pamplona for Spain, against Navarrese and French forces, who were in league to take it. Tiny Navarre was located between France and Spain, with important trade routes and deep culture; both Spanish and French monarchs believed that Navarre was essential to their long-term security. Their fights over Navarre had gone on for centuries.

The French wanted to free Navarre from Spanish hands. They even bought assistance from German mercenaries to aid them. But Spanish troops did not arrive in Pamplona as needed. They seem to have been diverted, perhaps mistakenly, elsewhere. So there were precious few soldiers at the castle with Iñigo to defend it. When the situation grew dire, all the soldiers wanted to surrender to the French and Navarrese—but not Iñigo. His sense of honor would not allow it. He also wasn't about to flee. His life mattered not at all compared to his dignity, and a soldier of honor does not abandon the cause or his comrades. So, he made his final confession and entered the battle on May 20, 1521, prepared to die for honor, fame, and God.

The story of what happened next is well known, the subject of many books and films. The cannonball that shattered Iñigo's leg was an improvement over the axes, spears, and maces that ravaged men's bodies throughout the battles of previous centuries. A cannon with its iron balls was, by contrast, a sophisticated, modern weapon. It was artillery shot from a distance, and it helped make hand-to-hand combat less necessary. Still, the effects could be devastating. They were devastating to Iñigo.

His right leg was destroyed by the cannonball, and his left leg wasn't exactly spared either. Surgeries on both came immediately afterward, the pain of which is difficult for someone in the twenty-first century to imagine. Leonardo da Vinci had recently dissected bodies, creating accurate drawings of human anatomy. Physicians used these in research, but mostly they used trial and error. Renaissance-era surgery was more like butchery. There was, of course, no anesthesia. Amputations were relatively easy, if rather unclean, and physicians often simply sealed the wound with hot oil where the incision had been made. But repairing bone was another matter.

Long after Iñigo had become known as Ignatius of Loyola, founder of the Society of Jesus, in his sixties when recounting these episodes to the scribe who penned his memoirs, Ignatius said of the Battle of Pamplona: "And so, with him [speaking of himself] falling, those in the stronghold then gave themselves up to the French." Of his surgeries he said, "He never spoke a word, nor showed any sign of pain other than clenching his fists tightly."[32] This wasn't pride. He was simply telling it like it was.

In the course of the initial two surgeries, he received last rites twice. Then, once he'd recovered slightly, after two surgeries came a third, cosmetic one to reset the leg yet again because it was noticeably shorter than the other, and also ugly and lumpy. He was disfigured, and for a man of his era and worldview, that was unbearable. After the procedure was done (cutting of bone without anesthesia), the account sounds like something straight out of a horror film, or the Spanish Inquisition: he regularly submitted to "stretching it . . . with appliances," saying, once again in the third person, and with more self-aggrandizing, "making a martyr of him."[33]

It was while recuperating, unable to move, that Iñigo began to read, not what he would have preferred—heroic tales and soldiering books—but the only two books on the shelves near where he lay incapacitated. Just imagine, wanting to read riveting, manly material, and all that you have at hand are *The Life of Christ* by a theologian named Ludolph of Saxony, consisting of long quotations from the Gospels and the church fathers, and a big book of lives of the saints, written 250 years earlier: *Legenda Aurea*, or *The Golden Legend*. These two books were there in the family home where Iñigo was recuperating because they were among the most popular books of that century among pious Catholics. Also, Iñigo's sister may have placed them in his room.

A generation earlier, Ludolph's *Life of Christ*, in addition to being a work of history and theology, had taught the religious and laypeople of the Devotio Moderna spiritual movement a kind of Christian meditation: how to imaginatively project oneself into a biblical scene and pray in that imaginative space. This approach was still revolutionary and new when Iñigo began to read the book in a Catalan edition. (It had been widely translated since first being published in 1472.) But only an Iñigo weakened by pain and suffering could have been ready to receive such devotional material. Ludolph of Saxony was a long way from what a man concerned with honor, armaments, and vanities might read. "Still," Ignatius dictated to the scribe later, "Our Lord was helping him, causing other thoughts, which were born of the things he was reading." Ludolph's book changed his life forever. "Until the age of twenty-six he was a man given up to the vanities of the world," said Ignatius, again speaking of himself, in his *Reminiscences*.[34]

Early in the pages of the other book, *The Golden Legend*, he found accounts of the lives and deaths of the four Evangelists. About St. Mark, Jacobus Voragine recorded: "When morning came, [the Romans] again put a rope around his neck and dragged him hither and yon, calling out: 'Haul the wild ox to the shambles!' As Mark was dragged along, he gave thanks, saying: 'Into your hands, O Lord, I commend my spirit,' and with these words he expired [as

Christ had done], in the reign of Nero." Voragine goes on to tell of how the Roman pagans wanted to burn the martyr's body, but lightning and hail poured down from heaven, scattering the fearful, "and Christians took [the body] away and buried it with all reverence in the church." The compilers of this history, as powerful as any knightly legend, follow this account with a simple description: "Saint Mark was a well-built man of middle age, with a long nose, fine eyes, and a heavy beard, balding and graying at the temples. He was reserved in his relations and full of the grace of God."[35] While reading these stories, the valiant soldier and aggressive seeker of fame, Iñigo, began to transform into a quieter man desirous of spiritual truth and divine contact. He began to look upon saints as having lives full of courage and grit, passion and endurance—worthy of any man's imitation, even his own.

# 7

## Old Battles and New Technologies

*Indulgences were as ubiquitous as the modern lottery ticket,*
*and indeed the earliest dated piece of English printing is a*
*template indulgence from 1476.*[36]
—Diarmaid MacCulloch

### The 1520s in Europe

While Iñigo was losing blood on the battlefield, Martin Luther's chief lieutenant for religious reform, Philipp Melanchthon, was publishing a picture book he had created with the help of Lucas Cranach, one of the era's most talented artists. Just as in our century it's often remarked that social media brings out the worst in people and is an outlet for giving bad inclinations a quick expression, so did new technology in the printing press, one of the great German inventions, encourage bad behavior among early-sixteenth-century Christians.

The midsized town of Wittenberg was a leader in the burgeoning book trade and publishing business. Obtaining its first printing press fifteen years before Luther's Ninety-Five Theses, this university city became the largest producer of books in all of Europe during Luther's lifetime—a title that it didn't relinquish until a half century after Luther's death.[37] Melanchthon and Cranach learned how to incite and communicate quickly from those who came before them. Like their mentor, Luther, they believed that they had a just and holy cause on their side. By the 1520s, Protestants widely understood the Reformation to be the unfolding of a global eschatological drama.

In wartime, Christians have always imagined that the end of eras was near. During the Gulf War of 1990–1991, there was a proliferation of apocalyptic and millenarian books for sale in bookstores. With their sensational covers picturing military jets and scenes from the Holy Land, these books played to the fears of Christians who believed that, given the geographical location of that conflict—close to the places where Jesus walked and where he is expected one day to return—it could be more than just a war. It could be the beginning of the Last Days. If we multiply those fears and anticipations by twenty, perhaps a thousand, we might be able to contemplate how ordinary Christians felt during the turbulence of the early sixteenth century.

First, the Hundred Years' War provided all the signs (according to oblique statements in the Old Testament book of Daniel and in the New Testament book of Revelation, interpreted to suit) of the Last Days. The Hundred Years' War lasted for five generations, fueling fears of the End Times, and it shaped the fears of Peter Faber's grandparents' generation. Then, when it ended and life seemed to return to normal, the year 1500 became the focus of fears and speculations. This turn of a century took place just six years before Peter's birth, and it rattled the Christian world. For example, these verses from the first book of John, which many readers of the time believed was written by the same man who penned Revelation and was the "beloved" disciple of Christ, featured prominently in popular literature:

> Love not the world, nor the things which are in the world. If any man love the world, the charity of the Father is not in him. For all that is in the world, is the concupiscence of the flesh. . . . And the world passeth away, and the concupiscence thereof: but he that doth the will of God, abideth for ever. Little children, it is the last hour; and as you have heard that Antichrist cometh, even now there are become many Antichrists: whereby we know that it is the last hour. (1 Jn. 2:15–18, Douay-Rheims)[38]

Ascetic purity, penitential acts, holy pilgrimages (including what was then an unusual, papal-decreed Jubilee Year, to sanction them), and apocalyptic preaching ("Repent!") were everywhere. Like Lucas Cranach, Albrecht Dürer, a well-known engraver and printmaker, in 1498 had created a series of prints called *Apocalypse with Pictures* that were sold and distributed in huge quantities and in many languages across Europe. These were the graphic novels of the time. Christians believed that the return of Christ to earth, the Last Judgment itself, was destined to come in the year 1500. When the world continued, despite the ominous year coming and going without any clear signs of divine intervention, a churchwide council was called in 1513 to forbid many of these ascetical activities under penalty of excommunication. This was just four years before Luther nailed his theses to the church door.

"Here was a pleasure widely shared among the many varieties of Protestantism," writes the history author Ferdinand Addis, "to come like Moses from the mountain against the cathedrals and monasteries of the false religion, to smash their painted windows and cast down the false idols and grind their precious images, their statues and their icons, into dust."[39] Philipp Melanchthon was twenty-four years of age in the spring of 1521 when Iñigo was on the battlefield in Pamplona. Luther had been formally excommunicated by the pope the previous January. The gloves were off on both sides of this religious and theological dispute. And young Melanchthon had learned well what visual art could do to communicate religious ideas from watching Dürer. He set out to smash whatever "false idols" he could of what he viewed as the false Roman religion.

Melanchthon titled his pamphlet *Passional Christi und Antichristi*, or *The Passion of Christ and the Antichrist*. Thirteen sets of woodcut images were designed to face the true Passion of Jesus Christ (on the left-hand page) against an imagined, satirized "passion" of Pope Leo X. These images could only be called caricatures. Printing presses and illustrated books had become not just a propaganda tool but what one expert has called "a true psychological revolution" for a public that was rapidly becoming literate and interested in printed material.[40] Many of the scenes of Leo X showed him taking money. Others named him as the Antichrist with a capital *A*; what had once been a vague medieval concept had come to refer to one person, the pope.

The reforming intentions of men such as Luther and Melanchthon had created a movement that was quickly styled with capital letters: the Reformation was fully born. So, then, did the rallying of the established church throughout Europe begin to call itself—also with due capitals—the Catholic

Church. *Catholic* means worldwide, one and only. Next, the argument became about legitimacy. Those calling themselves Protestants claimed to be the truly catholic ones. The measure for carrying the mantle of God's Word, they said, lay in faithfulness to theological principles that Protestants believed they were the inheritors of. Then, of course, it was that very presumption that led one Protestant group to become two, to become ten, to divide and subdivide among themselves like cells in a dish, splitting into more and more factions, over every conceivable point, principle, and practice.

*The Passion of Christ and the Antichrist* was the same size as one of today's trade paperbacks. It was the first illustrated attack of the young Reformation, published from the same Wittenberg where Luther had posted his Ninety-Five Theses on the door of the church at the center of the town four years earlier. The final spread of *The Passion of Christ and the Antichrist* shows Christ ascending to heaven and Pope Leo descending to hell. It was sold cheaply, like a handbill, on the streets.

On the one hand, the Reformation wasn't anything new. In other places in Europe, like Brussels and Prague, farther from the heart of the Holy Roman Empire, men and women, often supervised by renegade friars and other religious, had been celebrating free love and "down with church authority" for more than a century. One such group was the Adamites; they wanted a new Garden of Eden. On the other hand, there is something youthful and indiscreet about Melanchthon's book—as well as the fact that Luther wouldn't or couldn't disavow it. An intemperate prank became normative too quickly, and what may have started as the quieter complaints of an Augustinian monk and professor (Luther) quickly went from bombastic to sarcastic.

Luther's complaints *were* justified. The Roman Catholic Church *was* rife with corruption, clericalism, and greed. It *did* need reforming. In our own day, even Pope Francis has said as much, recalling what happened five hundred years ago while talking with reporters on the papal plane on June 26, 2016:

> The intentions of Martin Luther were not mistaken. He was a reformer. Perhaps some methods were not correct. But in that time . . . [t]here was corruption in the Church, there was worldliness, attachment to money, to power, and this he protested. . . . And today Lutherans and Catholics,

Protestants, all of us agree on the doctrine of justification. On this point, which is very important, he did not err. He made a medicine for the Church, but then this medicine consolidated into a state of things, into a state of a discipline, into a way of believing, into a way of doing, into a liturgical way and he wasn't alone; there was Zwingli, there was Calvin, each one of them different. . . . We must put ourselves in the story of that time. It's a story that's not easy to understand, not easy.

Pope Francis's tone in saying this was clearly filled with sadness and wistfulness for what might have been had other church leaders listened to the Augustinian friar's concerns. Pope Francis reiterated all of this again on October 31, 2016, while in Sweden to celebrate (yes, celebrate) the five-hundredth anniversary of the start of the Protestant Reformation. "Pope in Sweden Heaps Praise on Luther," read the headline on the Crux website the following day.

Luther's complaints about indulgences were not new, but his taking on the church from a position within (he was a respected friar and theology professor), was new. Number one of those ninety-five posted propositions set the stage for everything else: "When our Lord and Savior Jesus Christ said, 'Repent,' he willed that the entire life of believers be one of repentance." The other ninety-four might be considered almost unnecessary. Thirty-three-year-old Luther was confronting the very foundations of the Catholic Church—challenging its position as the necessary arbiter between men and God.

So, you see, when Iñigo de Loyola underwent his conversion to active faith, it took place in the context of a Catholicism under siege. Imagine how the seasoned soldier would have imagined his responsibilities, then. Still, Iñigo knew that he was done with violence, perhaps even fame.

"What new life is this we are beginning now?"[41] This is what Iñigo asked himself, over and over, in the early months of his conversion. After Pamplona, his three surgeries, and the sparking of religious interest in him while reading lives of the saints, he'd been inspired to become a pilgrim. But even after an extended stay at the Benedictine abbey of Montserrat in the Catalan mountains, obtaining a rough cassock for himself, giving his fancy clothes away to a beggar, standing all night in prayer, begging alms each day, making a general confession, and desiring to embark on the ultimate pilgrimage to the holy places of Jerusalem, his heart remained somewhat unconverted.

There was something romantic and chivalric in these early responses to his conversion—he started, after all, dreaming of knighthood and chivalry. First, there was the severe penance; second, the desire to combine penance with a trip to the Holy Land. When he was a young man, one of the great chivalric romances, *Tirant lo Blanc*, was published in Valencia, Spain. It begins like this:

> The knightly estate excels in such degree that it would be highly revered, if knights pursued the ends for which it was created. . . . In the rich, fertile, and pleasant isle of England lived Count William of Warwick, a brave knight of noble birth and even greater virtue who, through his wisdom and ingenuity, had served the cause of chivalry with great honor and whose fame had spread throughout the world. In his virile youth, this knight had often risked his life in battle, making war on land and sea and winning many jousts. He had bested seven kings and princes, leading armies of ten thousand, and had tilted in five great tournaments, always winning glorious victory.
>
> When this valiant count had reached the age of fifty-five, he was moved by divine inspiration to make a pilgrimage to the Holy Sepulcher in Jerusalem, which every Christian should visit to atone for his sins.[42]

In other words, Iñigo had begun to do his Martin of Tours, his Francis of Assisi, and a few other saint-imitating things, and he was pursuing his conversion with the same vigor with which he'd pursued his previous life of valor. But he was still unsure of where he was headed. Iñigo knew his heart remained unconverted from the embattled way he still felt: stuck between relishing prayer and hearing Mass, on the one hand, and evil spirits interesting him in his previous life, on the other hand.

In that period, many Christians felt at times assailed by evil spirits, demons, and unseen forces, in ways that may seem quaint or bizarre to people in the twenty-first century. The experience was not quaint or bizarre to them, though. It was immediate, terrifying, and urgent. That said, to Iñigo (and later, Faber), "discerning spirits" was something entirely greater. It was a task he would undertake deliberately as a part of his spiritual formation as a believer and as a follower of Jesus. We'll look in detail at this phenomenon in a later chapter. For now, the conflict within Iñigo of spirits both assailing and comforting him confused him greatly. It was saddening and frightening. This is why he kept saying to himself, "What new life is this we are beginning now?" And the understanding he'd soon come to, he would gift to his friend Faber as well.

# 8

# Roommates

What Peter Faber would discover in Paris would change him and then go on to have an impact on the world. Faber would discover who he was and for what he was created. This began in earnest when he met the first of the two Spaniards who would become his closest friends: the dandy Basque from Navarre, Francis Xavier. The two were acquainted within days of Faber's arrival in Paris. They quickly became university roommates.

Four years later, Faber met the other Spaniard, Iñigo de Loyola, who by then had traveled to Paris for schooling but also to escape the queries of Dominican friars of the Spanish Inquisition. As Mark Kurlansky playfully puts it in *The Basque History of the World*, "Silenced in Spain, he decided to put aside preaching and went to Paris, where his Basque ways and hybrid beliefs would have little chance of a following."[43]

As we've already seen, history has assigned Faber a secondary status to his more famous roommates. Peter stands in the background, as Francis Xavier and Ignatius of Loyola make headlines. The other two possessed a bearing of importance, like spiritual leaders with an air of authority. One imagines St. Paul at the Council of Jerusalem, or Swami Vivekananda just arrived in Chicago from India in 1893 to represent Hinduism at the World's Columbian Exposition—their physical bearing and voices couldn't possibly be ignored. In contrast, Peter was quiet in body and spirit. The difference between Faber and his two more famous friends rests, in part, on a certain natural humility in Peter. Xavier and Loyola were dark, gallant, and handsome; Faber was simple in appearance and demeanor. He wanted to blend in. The others also came from such different places; while Faber hailed from quiet mountains, they had dramatic stories to tell.

The University of Paris was a serious place for study—so serious, in fact, that some joked that it was more a prison than a school. Faber would soon learn that student life was difficult by any standard. There was little food, the water from the wells was unhealthy, and the students lived in damp chambers where standing water easily turned to ice throughout the winter months. One reason for these troubles was that credit was tough to come by, and Paris was an expensive city in which to live. Students were often lumped in with the poor as Parisians to be feared most of all, for they lived like vagabonds and had very little to lose. They even slept on straw beds. As one historian puts it, "Every student had to be attached to a college and submit to its discipline. Vagabond scholars, like the poor and the beggars, merged into the part of the population that inspired fear. They were susceptible to disorder and therefore must be contained."[44]

None of the letters exist that Faber would have written home to his parents in the Savoy, asking them to send money or telling them of his adventures. We do have a letter from Francis Xavier, Faber's first roommate, penned to his older brother, a nobleman in the Kingdom of Navarre, dated March 24, 1535, in which Xavier complains of his "sufferings and labors as a student" and adds details that offer a glimpse into student life:

> In your residence at Obanos, with every comfort round you, you feel the troubles of my watchings, and the difficulties with which I have to contend, as much as I feel them myself in Paris. . . . I am often without the necessaries of life, for no other reason, I feel certain, than that your unfailing readiness to come to my aid has not been sufficiently informed as to the numberless wants which I suffer—wants, the particulars of which sound, for the most part, minute and insignificant when spoken of, but which are yet very hard to bear.[45]

Both the melodrama and the hardship are characteristic of what most students in Paris commonly experienced. Like Xavier, they were often writing home, asking for money.

In addition to familiar financial hardships, which follow students in every time and place, these were also days when young men would begin to explore the world in ways they hadn't been able to back home. This often included carousing and women. But sixteenth-century mores surrounding correction and punishment were different from our own, and students in Faber's university days were routinely whipped for these offenses, as well as for much smaller ones, such as missing curfew.

Faber would come to love it all. His pursuit was the trivium, the traditional foundation of every good liberal arts education: grammar, dialectic, and rhetoric. This involved intensive study of Plato and Aristotle and Boethius, as well as logic and the art of argument. Later would come the quadrivium of arithmetic, astronomy, geometry, and music. More than half his time in school would be spent learning Latin and Greek, and immersing oneself in these ancient languages was also the means by which a university student learned about the past. There were no classics, then, or what today we call "history." History, rather, was found in the languages and the writings of the Latin and Greek classics. Also different from today's education was the function of memory. Memory was an essential part of learning. Faber would have memorized long portions of the works in Latin and Greek as part of learning them. Thus, one became intimate with the tone and tenor, the nuance and spirit, of the past.

Faber read a lot of ancient and medieval philosophy, but these were read differently from how they are read by students of philosophy today. In the early sixteenth century, reading philosophy meant logic, grammar, rhetoric, and Latin and Greek readings in Aristotle, Cicero, Augustine, Peter Lombard, Abelard, and Thomas Aquinas. Whereas a textbook today in medieval philosophy would include a large section, perhaps its opening section, on arguments for the existence of God, such a question was backbone to all learning in Faber's day. It was not a separate, let alone leading, topic of concern or study. So, when philosophy students today turn to Augustine, Anselm, and Duns Scotus for the classic evidences that God exists, in Faber's time these "proofs" were not of great importance.

The Collège Sainte-Barbe was more interested in what today we call the humanities. The new humanism that was the core of the curriculum, as well as the ethos of the Collège, would serve Faber well throughout his life. Geography was rapidly changing at the time, and men and women were anxiously learning about new peoples and cultures, realizing that their fields of knowledge were not as conclusive as their parents and grandparents had once imagined them to be. Faber's university experience grounded him in understanding and appreciating the differences among people.

God's existence was assumed in a way that colored the rest of the curriculum. Topics such as God's physics (on light, on magnets, on free-falling bodies), God's logic (propositions, insolubles), and knowledge of God (on being, on immortality and soul, on the Trinity) occupied the minds of curious students. For example, imagine the excitement that Peter felt when he heard his first lecture on Robert Grosseteste's treatise "On Light." Grosseteste was an early-thirteenth-century priest, bishop, theologian, philosopher, and scientist—a professor at Oxford. He taught the subject of the primordial moment of Creation, according to the account in Genesis. But he didn't dwell on the Bible—he simply knew that his readers and students would know that "In the beginning . . . God said, 'Let there be light'"—and this was before the creation of the sun, moon, and stars. How provocative, then, that he also said, "Light is a form entirely inseparable from matter," and how fascinating that from light comes all generation and motion.

A treatise like "On Light" was to Faber's generation what Einstein's papers on relativity might be to today's students—except that the analogy breaks down when one considers how little of higher education is shared among students today. We go to many different schools and, in a world where information has increased exponentially compared to Faber's era, are encouraged early to specialize in a specific discipline; thus, a brilliant student at university today might never be asked to encounter the writings of Einstein. In contrast, at the University of Paris in the 1520s, every student was challenged with the same core of study and knowledge.

## Back to the Classics

More than two centuries had passed since Thomas Aquinas had "baptized" Aristotle into Catholic theology throughout his voluminous *Summa Theologica*. Two centuries also had passed since the bishop of Paris, in 1270, four years before Aquinas's death, condemned certain propositions from Aristotle's books on natural philosophy, which they called science. By the time Faber was a student in Paris, Aristotle was so established in the teaching of the church that Luther felt it necessary to make one of his famous Ninety-Five Theses read: "Virtually the entire *Ethics* of Aristotle is the worst enemy of grace." Really? What was wrong with Aristotle?

Luther believed that the Scholastic use of Aristotle, who lived before Christ and had never heard of grace, had resulted in Christians forgetting about the role of grace in forgiveness. Just before posting his theses, Luther said this in lectures he delivered on St. Paul's letter to the Romans: "It is mere madness for them to say that a man of his own powers is able to love God above all things and to do the works of the law in substance . . . without grace. Fools! Theologians for swine!"[46] He was no diplomat.

At the same time, Luther was himself a humanist of sorts, encouraging ordinary people to challenge authority and think for themselves. Even sacred doctrines that were held in awe and wonder, handed down by the magisterium, were the subject of Luther's arguments and even scorn. Four years later, Luther's ally, Philipp Melanchthon, would add in one of his theology books, *Loci Communes* (Latin for "common ground," meaning "fundamentals"), that "the Church embraced Aristotle instead of Christ." That was the problem as Protestants saw it with what had become essential teaching in universities—and for clergy—for a couple of centuries.

The eighth and ninth books of Aristotle's *Nicomachean Ethics*, on friendship, formed the backbone of Renaissance moral theory in the 1520s. At times, the pagan philosopher even sounds like one who has been enlightened by the Gospel—for instance, when he explains that nothing is as important as the virtue of friendship: "Friendship seems too to hold states together, and lawgivers to care more for it than for justice; for concord seems to be something like friendship, and this they aim at most of all, and expel factions as their worst enemy; and when men are friends they have no need of justice."[47] Saints like Francis of Assisi would cheer at this, had they known it, the language is so familiar.

It was from the *Nicomachean Ethics* that Faber learned the nobility of friendship, the essentialness of loving and caring for oneself in friendship, friendship's reciprocity, its ability to build community, and even the right occasions for breaking off friendship. Aristotle said that there were friendships of utility, of pleasure, but most important were those friendships inspired by virtue. Faber also learned, through Thomas Aquinas's interpretation of Aristotle's *Ethics*, that there is a friendship with God, one that was even glimpsed by the ancient philosopher, and some kinds of friendship might transcend what is normally possible in human nature.

Aristotle on friendship prepared Faber, too, to understand how friends can come together in a common cause for good. The eighth book of *Nicomachean Ethics* explains, "Perfect friendship is the friendship of men who are good, and alike in virtue; for these wish well alike to each other *qua* good, and they are good in themselves." Such men are useful to each other, the philosopher explains; they are good; they are pleasant and enjoyable to be around; they possess qualities that complement each other; they resemble each other in virtue and in deed. "But it is natural," Aristotle says, "that such friendships should be infrequent; for such men are rare."[48] Faber would carry these lessons with him throughout his life.

# 9

# Falling in Love: Iñigo's Influence

*They and only they can acquire . . . the sacred power of self-intuition, who*
*within themselves can interpret and understand the symbol, that the wings*
*of the air-sylph are forming within the skin of the caterpillar.*[49]
—Samuel Taylor Coleridge

## October–December 1529

The greatest gift in Faber's life was a natural gratefulness. He was born to good, Catholic parents, by God's grace. He felt the freedom to leave his country to pursue his studies with fervor, by God's grace. There was no sense in Faber of having earned the gifts in his life. He saw them as what they were: divine gifts. Such a benevolent sincerity others must have envied. Likewise, Faber would view his meeting Iñigo de Loyola as an incredible blessing and one that would forever alter the course of his life. Faber writes, "Eternally blessed be all this that divine providence arranged for my good and for my salvation."[50]

Iñigo came to share rooms with Peter and Xavier in the fall of 1529. In contrast to the two teenagers, Iñigo had already experienced more of life than most men do in a lifetime. He'd been a courtier, a gentleman, a soldier, and then a religious pilgrim—all this before he ever became a student. Iñigo took to Xavier immediately. They were similar in background and temperament. Royal born, Xavier was Iñigo's countryman, from Navarre, the territory of northern Spain that borders the Basque Country to one side and Aquitaine, France, to the north. It has been the subject of a nearly ancient tug-of-war between the two countries, and Xavier experienced much of that even as a child. The capital city of Navarre was Pamplona—the very city that Iñigo de

Loyola helped to defend, almost to his own demise, when Xavier was just a boy.

Faber was, probably, by contrast a puzzle to the ex-soldier. Faber was still talking about becoming a monk and completely uncertain as to what he might do with his life. He was uncertain about many things, including himself, in contrast to the Spaniard Xavier in the next room. A man of strong character who already possessed a lifetime of experiences, an ex-soldier and gracious courtier, Iñigo was also a new student and needed help with his Greek and philosophy. Faber became his tutor, and each week they sat and studied Aristotle. One imagines those afternoons with Faber opening books to Iñigo, and Iñigo, flashing eyes and dramatic gestures, revealing a world-worn wisdom to the boy from the Savoy. Faber reflected years later, "For after providence decreed that I was to be the holy man's instructor, and we conversed about secular matters, then we talked of spiritual things."[51]

Iñigo was under the influence of the convicting Spirit of God. Before arriving at university, he'd spent the summer begging on the streets of Flanders. His desire for penance and his sense of asceticism were, by all accounts and renderings, intense—more intense than the desire of those around him. He liked to imitate the saints precisely, as when he stripped himself naked in front of a poor man, exchanging clothes with him—like St. Martin of Tours, or Francis of Assisi. Or, when he spent the entire night in prayer, standing, so as not to fall asleep—like St. Simeon Stylites.[52] He was a spiritual pilgrim, a mendicant, and a vowed religious, but without an order. Faber, too, remembered the private vows that he had made himself years earlier.

Iñigo was seeking to turn others around, as well, sometimes even by resorting to clandestine tactics, as when he learned that a friend was frequently using the services of a prostitute. This friend wouldn't take seriously Iñigo's appeals to virtue, or to the salvation of his soul, so Iñigo hid under a bridge upon which the friend would routinely rendezvous. As his friend made his way to the middle of the bridge one night, suddenly he heard a deep voice calling out, "Go, unhappy man, and enjoy your filthy pleasures, while I stay here doing penance for you, if perchance I may avert from you the just vengeance of God!"[53]

When Iñigo spoke, every person in a café or classroom would turn to look and listen. He possessed that kind of a voice. He had that sort of *presence*. And he was older and wiser than his new roommates. But it wasn't how Iñigo spoke that drew Faber to him. There were times when what the older man said seemed to penetrate through Peter's self-doubt straight to his heart. Iñigo told Faber of how often he wept during Mass, of how he sought to be humble in love, not fear, of God, and of the contentment and delight in his soul. From the start, theirs was not a typical relationship between sixteenth-century men, founded in strength with tests of masculinity. It was as if this new friend possessed precisely what Faber had been searching for all those years.

Faber didn't need to be convicted of any particular sin, as did some of the men Iñigo was talking with those first months in Paris. Faber hadn't lived enough by then to really sin—but he was guilty of diminishing himself and making too much of what sin he had indeed committed. To recognize this, and seek forgiveness for it, can be more difficult than recovering from particular wickedness. Iñigo could understand immediately. Faber was guilty of doubting the presence of God in his life. He became Iñigo's tutor in philosophy and classics, and Iñigo became Peter's tutor in matters of the soul.

When someone says that he has found the secret to the purpose of human living—that he's experienced a transformation in his life as a result—you pay attention. And that is exactly what happened next.

## The Secret to Knowing God

Iñigo showed Faber something he'd been working on: the result of years of personal prayer and contemplation. It was unlike anything Faber had heard in catechism or in the teachings of friars, priests, and professors he'd been listening to for years. Iñigo would eventually come to call the work his *Spiritual Exercises*. Creating the exercises was the passion and practice that filled him and was most essential to his life.

To Faber, Iñigo was explaining how he had fallen in love with God in Christ. Love was a familiar topic of conversation of young men in dormitories, but not like this. Iñigo was also recording the activity of his soul daily—another thing Peter had never encountered. Feelings, emotions, and desires were all taken as God-inspired. Listening to such intangibles was essential to understanding what God wanted. To say "I experienced deep longings" became a way of expressing a gift of divine insight. Iñigo explained that the purpose of prayer is to draw upon and develop the life that faith, by God's grace, has deposited in us. Faber—like most people who encounter this teaching for the first time—was bowled over. He was discovering for the first time the inner life of faith.

"On January 10, 1529, at the age of twenty-three, I became a bachelor of arts and after Easter was awarded the licentiate under Master Juan de la Pena,"[54] wrote Faber years later in his account of these years. All the while, he was listening to Iñigo wherever they went. Combining gifts for conversation (the "gift of gab") and personal passion, Iñigo had added genius in blending fidelity to Mother Church, a commitment to learning and discovery, and a strong sense of responsibility. Soon, not just Faber but a cohort of men became active contemplatives around their leader. They were all earnest Catholics, students of tradition, and adventurous in spirit. They were ascetics who wanted to live in the real world. Soon, they would become a puzzle to the leaders of the existing religious orders of their day and to many who were in places of ecclesiastical power.

Iñigo taught Faber how to relate to his sin in useful ways. Iñigo had experienced a conversion of several dramatic kinds. He'd personally progressed from blustering arrogance to submissiveness, at least to Mother Church. He'd gone from violent and vengeful in his relationships to a deliberate desire to live by the Beatitudes. He had been a man who wooed women and "won" them over but was now trying to live by a vow of chastity. The sacrament of confession is to credit for changing Iñigo's heart. He knew as much, and so he introduced the sacrament to Faber—who made a general confession and then made it his practice to go once each week.

Just as important, Iñigo taught Peter a spiritual practice that he'd begun to refine and utilize with precision in his own life. It is called the daily Examen, a word in Latin that means simply "examination." The Examen is a spiritual practice that one does entirely with oneself, but in those days it began when Ignatius would show it to someone. As Faber says, "To help me [prepare for going to confession], Iñigo gave me the daily examination of conscience."[55] Then and now, when praying the Examen, the person is asked, usually at day's end, to pause and examine his or her life and experience that day. The Examen looks like this:

1. Place yourself in God's presence. Give thanks for God's great love for you.

2. Pray for the grace to understand how God is acting in your life.

3. Review your day—recall specific moments and your feelings at the time.

4. Reflect on what you did, said, or thought in those instances. Were you drawing closer to God, or further away?

5. Look toward tomorrow—think of how you might collaborate more effectively with God's plan. Be specific, and conclude with the "Our Father."[56]

"He gave me an understanding of my conscience," Faber recounts, before naming temptations and sins he had committed in his imagination—specifically, fornication. "I would gladly have gone to a desert and eaten herbs and roots only, forever," Faber says, "if it weren't for the remedy Ignatius provided."[57] That remedy was not one, but four: make a general confession to a priest introduced to Faber by Iñigo; then, go to confession weekly; go to communion weekly; and learn the Examen—this daily, personal examination of conscience, which has been a centerpiece of the Jesuit way ever since these founding members of the Society of Jesus began doing it together five hundred years ago. These were all tangible spiritual practices to be followed with earnest deliberation.

With this attention on his soul, other issues bubbled up. Anxiety and worry were floundering in Faber's out-of-shape soul, as his life was at that time without focus or purpose. He often thought he was depressed. Other times, bored. The French call it *ennui*. By way of a remedy, Iñigo showed him how to be a follower of Jesus each day.

Iñigo was a master psychologist. He understood people in a way that was unlike anything Peter had encountered. His approach came at just the right time in Faber's life: when he was dying of thirst. *Give me something to drink,* Peter thought, *or I'm going to wither.* He was confused. "I was always unsure of myself and blown about by many winds: sometimes wishing to be married, sometimes to be a doctor, sometimes a lawyer, sometimes a lecturer, sometimes a professor of theology, at others, a monk," Faber remembers.

## Spiritual Experience and the Soul

But most of all, there were the *Spiritual Exercises*. A few philosophical words and definitions are necessary before we continue.

At this time in the history of the church, the dominant theological world-view of the late Middle Ages—the path worn by Anselm, Bernard of Clairvaux, Dominic, and the Dominicans including St. Thomas Aquinas—was called realism, which taught the existence and importance of universal truths and principles. This was beginning to change, however. Essential to Iñigo and Faber was, in contrast to the outlook of traditional realism, individual experience. Personal experience was a gift of grace from God and essential to understanding oneself and God. Such a way of looking at the world wouldn't have been possible if others hadn't made inroads into philosophical realism in the century before Iñigo and Faber were born.

This alternative theological view was called nominalism, and in its practical forms it should be understood not as a denial of realism but as a new emphasis on the particularities of existence that are important for human understanding. For Iñigo and Faber, discovering Christ in the Spiritual Exercises, the truths of the realists become understandable and more real through the particularities of confession, the daily Examen, contemplation, meditation, and prayer.

One didn't have to study at the Sorbonne in Paris to discover the writings of Aquinas. Everyone with an interest in theology, like Faber, knew "Friar Thomas," the thirteenth-century master. Aquinas was declared a saint within fifty years of his death and was already *the* doctor of the doctors of the church. Faber knew, according to St. Thomas, that "although a human soul can subsist by itself it hasn't a complete specific nature of its own." And he knew that "the soul is joined to a body for its own perfection, both its essential perfection—the completion of its species—and a supervening perfection—the knowledge it draws from the senses, for this is the human being's natural mode of understanding."[58] But, how?

The Spiritual Exercises was not the first prayer retreat/program in which a practitioner of prayer encouraged directees to use their imaginations in prayer practice. There had been others since the Franciscan and Dominican orders were established three centuries earlier. Particularly, St. Bonaventure (1221–1274), the theologian minister-general of the Franciscans, offered in his *Life of Christ* almost "a prototype of the *Exercises*: readers should 'consider,' 'meditate,' 'contemplate,' and 'render themselves present' to the biblical scenes.'"[59] Iñigo learned from him and from others.

The Exercises were designed to foster an experience of prayer. Catholics had been praying for fifteen centuries, of course. The liturgy had long before been established with a core of written prayers that were deemed essential for every faithful Catholic. There was no lack of reciting prayers, both in and out of church, particularly since St. Dominic or one of his contemporaries was given the prayers of the holy rosary in the thirteenth century, then added to the prayer tool chest of every Catholic. There were also the *Memorare*—seeking the intercession of the Blessed Virgin Mary—and the *Anima Christi*, which begins "Soul of Christ, sanctify me," among others commonly known and prayed.

But what Iñigo realized was that the experience of prayer was another matter entirely, different from the recitation of words, no matter how holy those words might be. Such experience was uncommon, he knew from his own attempts, and he wanted to show his fellow Catholics how to open themselves up to God's grace in ways that allowed an experience of the holy to permeate what otherwise might be a much drier way of being faithful.

It was with these desires and for these purposes that he developed his deceptively simple Exercises. They were not dissimilar from medieval ways of contemplation upon holy mysteries that included focusing on the themes of the Passion of Christ—but they expanded these methods, and their impact on the future of Christian spirituality would be immense. There are parallels, in fact, between Iñigo's psychological and spiritual work and the discoveries of modern psychology. Both focus on repression as nearly universal in human experience. And both insist that the past exists in the present. A modern therapist will guide a patient to discover what lies behind a subconscious attempt to avoid reality, or substitute for or sublimate it, and Iñigo asked that a person undertaking the Exercises essentially do the same. Both the spiritual director and the modern therapist will guide a novice to listen carefully to his or her loves. They share an understanding of mystical connection that's rooted in the affections. Centuries of puritanical reaction against such ancient, deeply biblical notions have obscured this understanding—but to the first Jesuits the human situation was clear: the passion, affection, and loves that bubble inside of us, moving us toward things and people, are there for divine reasons. These passions, affections, and loves can be discovered and put to good use in one's life.

It was risky to one's soul to experiment in the ways of the Spiritual Exercises. In our day, the word *spiritual* has become so overused and meaningless that we perhaps have trouble seeing anything with *spiritual* modifying it as being exciting. In Latin, they were called *Exercitia spiritualia*, and that begins to suggest what might happen. The Spiritual Exercises were risky, even strange, to most Christians. For a set period of time, divided into "weeks" that were sequential movements rather than chronological segments, a participant set out to discover God's will for his life. In itself, such a program was not new. However, Iñigo's method for discovery involved the imagination, even to the point of role play, and so immediately one was dabbling in mystical work with Christ. It seemed presumptuous to many to "look" for Jesus and "listen" for his voice, but that was the training: to use the physical senses. The Exercises took most seriously the notion that God is living and active and wanting to be known by his followers. Heretics, however, made claims not unlike those being made by Iñigo—to special knowledge of God—and this made Iñigo's process appear risky to some.

Faber was already a passionate, intelligent young man, and now he was being asked to pray the Exercises for the first time. He was unsure of himself, and he felt absorbed in sin and need for God. As a Jesuit who teaches literature to college students has recently explained: "Ignatius understood that our imagination held the physical and the spiritual together, that God was revealed to us in our imaginations, allowing us to ground our aspirations and desires, in all their particularities, within the reality of Christ's call to live free and full lives."[60]

These ways of using and honoring the gift of imagination to know God would later—in the generations after Faber's death—led Jesuits to create a thriving ministry of theater at Jesuit-run universities throughout Europe. Again, their work surprised people. These theatrical productions were unlike any others that people had experienced: "There were trap-doors for ghost apparitions and vanishing acts, flying machines and cloud apparatus. On every conceivable occasion, the Jesuit producers made divinities appear in the clouds, ghosts rise up and eagles fly over the heavens, and the effect of these stage tricks was further enhanced by machines producing thunder and the noise of winds."[61] Again, all the senses were brought to bear as people were shown how to find and see God all around them.

This discovering of Jesus in the imagination was, for Faber, a discovery of a kind of love—so much so that he would write with regret that he hadn't been schooled in this spiritual experience years earlier. "The Lord and spouse of my soul willed to take possession of me," he said, referring to his youth before he left for Paris. "If only I had known, I would have known, I would have brought him in order to follow him, so as never to be separated from him again!"[62] Peter was talking about Jesus as a person in love might talk of his beloved.

Iñigo showed Peter that the Exercises are organized into four "weeks." A person asks for grace each week, beginning in what is called, in the language of Ignatian spirituality, the First Week, for light from God to reveal what most needs changing and healing in one's life, as well as a deepening of desire to make those changes. Peter delved deeply into the First Week. One is instructed to focus on personal sin and one's need for healing from sin, guilt, fear, and even poor self-image. This was the heart of Peter's spiritual struggles, and he spent that first week mostly alone (one doesn't talk to a soul), fasting and attempting to live in the cold, without a fire, in the middle of a Paris winter. These impulses—all of them—were some of the reasons he and Iñigo had personally connected so quickly. Faber had been filled with a yearning for God since childhood and with a desire to search his heart that had gone unfulfilled. His friend knew him well already. Now, Peter began to learn that the way to find God was to listen in his heart for what he most desired—but only after he could come to terms with his feelings of guilt and self-doubt.

The Second Week is a focusing on the person of Jesus: to find oneself with him, look upon him, listen to him, in scenes from the Gospels. Only then, after imaginatively being present with the Lord, does one choose whether to follow him. The Third Week and Fourth Week intensify this fresh commitment as the pray-er imagines the Passion of Christ, reflects again and now more deeply upon sin and the meaning of sin in a relationship with Christ, and then, contemplating the profound love of God, chooses again to respond to that love with one's life.

After Peter completed the Exercises once, he soon completed them twice, and soon began teaching them to others, with Iñigo's full blessing. Iñigo, in fact, said that Peter understood the Exercises and could teach them to others better than anyone else. Soon, with his encouragement, Faber was studying to become a deacon, then a priest. He was ordained a subdeacon that February of 1534, a deacon by April, and said his first Mass on July 22, 1534. He was only twenty-eight.

It was as if Peter had reached up and stretched his arms and legs for the first time. He was becoming who he was destined to become. God had made him for precisely this. He would always remain in the shadows of Iñigo and Francis Xavier. That, he understood. But as most any Jesuit will tell you, Peter is the saint to whom they most often turn for guidance today. Faber may not be the Francis of Assisi of the Jesuits—he wasn't the original inspiration for the order—but he was truly the cofounder and, according to many, he was the heart behind the original charism. It is typical, for instance, that the spiritual path of Ignatius and Peter became known simply as "Ignatian," named only for one of them.

Iñigo would eventually come to be known throughout the world according to the Latinized version of his name written on his degree upon graduating in Paris: Ignatius of Loyola, and that is how we will refer to him most often from here on. Much of the history of the Jesuits in the sixteenth century can be traced back to student housing in Paris shared by these three. Xavier and Ignatius were canonized on the same day in 1622. Where was Faber, then? He would have to wait nearly four more centuries.

## Heading to Montmartre

At the end of more than four years in Paris, by the summer of 1533, Faber had been resolved, he tells us, "to try to follow Iñigo in a life of poverty." It was then that he returned home across the Alps to see his family, one more time. Some of these roads are paved now, but even so, they are counted among the most dangerous to drive in all the world. The hairpin turns can be terrifying.[63] On this fateful occasion, Faber arrived after a long journey only to find that his mother was dead. He stayed for seven months, surely talking with his father about his future plans, potential careers, and what Peter wanted for himself. Physician, lawyer, lecturer, secular priest (not a member of a religious order)—these were the usual possibilities, often contemplated for him at home, we know from Faber's journal. But now, what would he do with his life? Monastic life was a possibility; Peter had thought about it. A monastery like Cluny or Saint-Denis would provide him with a lifetime of security, companionship, libraries, and satisfying work.

By early 1534, Faber returned to Paris, again on those mountain passes, but this time as an adult knowing who he was. He was, as he put it, "settled upon the course of my life through the help given me by God through Iñigo."[64] Faber was still just twenty-eight.

His commitments to family satisfied, without compunction Faber moved quickly with Ignatius into formal religious life. The time for private commitments and university late-night conversations was soon to be past. In rapid succession upon his return, Faber made the Exercises, the first of the friends of Ignatius to do so, and was then ordained subdeacon, deacon, then priest, the last of these on May 30. He celebrated his first Mass on the Feast of Mary

Magdalene, with great intention, always conscious of his own faults, looking to her as an advocate for sinners everywhere.

That summer would witness the founding of what would come to be called the Society of Jesus.

It was a typically tumultuous spring and summer in Europe. Much of the tumult was religiously inspired. In the north, in Münster, Westphalia (now Germany), an Anabaptist enclave had just been founded where its clergy declared the place the New Jerusalem, the place of Christ's Second Coming, and began forcibly baptizing anyone who was not in agreement. In France, Protestants (who wouldn't be known as Huguenots, a name that probably most closely meant "confederates," until a generation later, after Faber's death) began to publicly denounce the Catholic Mass as superstitious, provoking outrage and physical confrontations between people, even within families. In England, Sir Thomas More was confined to the Tower of London upon the order of King Henry VIII. That fall, the English Parliament would pass the Act of Supremacy, making Henry VIII, not the pope, the supreme head over the Church of England. Thomas More would go on trial for treason the following summer and be beheaded.

On August 15, 1534, on the Feast of the Assumption, when Faber, Ignatius, Xavier, and four other of the first members of the Society of Jesus met in the crypt of the Chapel of Saint-Denis on Montmartre, just north of Paris, and took their first vows together, the first and only priest among them was Father Faber. He's the one who celebrated Mass, which means that he would have faced the altar and taken the sacrament before handing it to his friends. Symbolic of his leadership, it is clear from every account that, for him at least, priesthood was always and only about service.

Each of the men present had, that summer, before the August 15 event, completed the Spiritual Exercises, as Peter had back in January and February. Had they not, Ignatius believed, they might not have been prepared to make the decision they were making that day to follow Christ.

Faber took on a leadership role. When Ignatius was away—as he soon was for health reasons, or on missions of various kinds—Peter became the cohort leader. Soon he became interested in the need for reform throughout the church, particularly after meeting a few local reformers. Nothing changed Faber like relationships. Nothing was ever more important to him than friendships. Preachers and teachers like Luther, Calvin, and Melanchthon were in the news and denounced from Catholic lecterns and pulpits from Lisbon to Venice, but Faber began to know their stories. He sought out their followers and would soon be asking for permission to seek out the reformers themselves to talk with them.

# 10

## Interlude: "Bless the Lord, O my soul, and do not forget all his benefits."

Faber's memoir, *Memoriale*, is a secret gem in the history of Christian spirituality, read by so few people over the past five centuries, so rarely translated, and even more rarely published, that it is familiar to almost no one outside the Jesuit order. Yet it may just be one of the most powerful, revealing, and significant Christian books ever written.

When he comes to write *Memoriale*, Faber begins by quoting two verses from the opening of Psalm 103 and truncates them in a way that shows his simple, no-fuss approach to faith. He was always more practical than pious or theological, and he was certainly "a mystic, not an ascetic," as Pope Francis characterized him and Ignatius of Loyola in an interview.[65]

Faber also writes in a 1544 letter about his "principles for the pursuit of perfection," listing as the first two: "Overcome yourself. Abide within yourself." This paradox would be key to his spiritual vision.

Many of his contemporaries were occupied with personal acts of asceticism—beating up their bodies was their religion. The pious often wore hair shirts. Priests and confessors were sometimes asked by penitents to flog their shoulders with chains. Even counts and kings would sometimes demonstrate—to themselves, to God, and to anyone looking—their sincerity by having servants scourge them, prod them, or pull them by ropes around their necks. This was not Faber's way to God at all.

When Faber writes about himself, the tone is different from these others, and even different from the ways that his friend, Ignatius, wrote about himself.

For example, Ignatius easily points to his own virtues (again, he speaks of himself in the third person), as in this passage about his preparation for traveling to Jerusalem in 1523: "Although some people were offering to accompany him, he didn't want to go except alone. . . . Thus one day, when some people were really pressing him to take a companion . . . he told them that, even if it were the son of the brother of the Duke of Cardona, he wouldn't go in his company. For he wanted to have three virtues: charity and faith and hope." Ignatius goes on to explain that, if he traveled with someone, he'd end up relying on that person in times of hunger or exhaustion and so on, but instead he would put all his hope and trust in God alone. Similarly, when talking of his own commitment to poverty, Ignatius seems to almost revel in the details, as when he boards a ship in Venice to travel to the Holy Land, before meeting Faber, and recounts: "Onto this ship too he brought nothing with which to feed himself beyond the hope he was placing in God."[66] How grand all of this seems, at least compared to the life of Faber. And this is one of the reasons Faber appeals to some today more than his famous friend does.

Faber speaks plainly of travel and its difficulties, always without spiritual aggrandizement. He is always gesturing away from himself in *Memoriale*, referring to God, or attendant angels, saints of the places he was visiting, or the people to whom he was trying to minister. This is the context for appreciating Faber's plain quoting of the psalm. It is one of those statements of spiritual sentiment that is, in fact, so simple as to be easily overlooked: "Bless the Lord, O my soul, and do not forget all his benefits." That's what Faber simply did.

# 11

## Vocation Found

*It would be well, and proper, and obedient, and pure, to grasp your one necessity and not let it go.*
—Annie Dillard

### 1530–Spring 1534

At Iñigo's encouraging, not only did Faber steer his course away from law, the monastery, and the academy to become a simple priest: he also began to overcome the depression that had plagued him his whole life.

Much has been made of Faber's depression over the years, including by some of the experts in the Society of Jesus who have studied his life. In the way that Faber himself describes it, his depression was not necessarily a disease. He calls his "bouts of depression" times of worry, fear, and hesitation, which are certainly not unusual, and even, one might say, frequently healthy responses to life's challenges. But he also seems to have suffered from a mild nervous condition. Was depression a sin in his life? Probably not, but then, that was a matter for Faber and his confessor to discern. It was certainly debilitating to him at times, according to Faber's descriptions, and was probably a condition or state that would be given a formal diagnosis today, along the spectrum of mental or nervous disorders.

Faber thanks God in his memoirs that, after Iñigo's spiritual interventions, these bouts never lasted for more than three days at a time. And thirteen years after earning his licentiate to teach from the university, remembering how depression and its kin, indecision, plagued him, Peter offers this advice to others: "Sometimes timidity and weakness of spirit can weaken our bodies.

Conversely, robustness of mind can make our bodies robust. Hence, in our toils we ought to throw aside all fear, timidity, and so forth. The spirit will bear up our bodies."[67]

He speaks of gluttony, too, with a tone of struggle and regret, as a repeated sin in his life that needed to be conquered. A lack of charity toward others, too. Peter accuses himself and reflects that Christ has helped him overcome it. The source of all these burdens and sins was what Peter and other early Jesuits called "bad" or "evil spirits." This is one of the great lessons they learned from Ignatius.

A significant portion of the *Spiritual Exercises* is taken up with "Rules for the Discernment of Spirits" (paragraphs 313–36). As someone who was actively and earnestly trying to purge his sins, Faber discovered in these teachings that his evil spirits were likely to cause in him "gnawing anxiety" to "sadden [him], and to set up obstacles." Often, the obstacles are reasons that the evil spirits will suggest for why a soul needs progress toward holiness. It is the role of the good spirits, then, "to stir up courage and strength, consolations, tears, inspirations, and tranquility. He makes things easier and eliminates all obstacles, so that the persons may move forward in doing good."[68]

Significantly, where most morality lessons throughout history since Plato had taught that desire was something to be overcome by better parts of the mind and soul, Ignatius learned that desires are not necessarily bad. Desires don't have to lead us to sin. Desire, in and of itself, in fact, is good, Ignatius taught Faber. Imaginings, revulsions, and impulses all come from the same place. Ignatius taught what was counterintuitive in Christianity at that time: a Christian needn't focus on damping down his or her desires but should reorder them toward what is good. For example, if one follows a desire such as lust, the problem is not just the sin (the lusting) but also the superficiality of the desire. "What greater desires God has intended for us!" Ignatius would have said.

This all takes place inside us. There are "motions caused in the soul" by good and bad spirits, Ignatius said. The important thing is to be able to discern good from bad. A good spirit brings with it love, joy, peace, but also sadness and restlessness, causing one to reexamine one's life. In other words, a good spirit can be one that doesn't necessarily feel good but is good for you. An evil spirit most often brings with it confusion and doubt; it also may prompt a feeling of contentment or laziness that discourages change that would be good for the soul. "Enemies of our human nature," Ignatius called the ways of the flesh, the influence of the devil, and the bad spirits in the world around us. This principle is very much in line with the ancient human understanding (going back again at least to the ancient Greeks) of good and bad impulses residing inside us, pulling us in two directions: toward good, but at the same time toward bad.

Faber flourished under Ignatius's direction.

Methods of spiritual discernment were nothing new in Catholicism, and there were varied traditions for how to obtain personal illumination. In fact, mystics before Ignatius had talked so much about these things that Luther saw fit to rail against them in one of his treatises, sarcastically referring to mysticism as "God's new sublime art, taught by the heavenly voice, which we at Wittenberg, who teach faith and love, do not understand and cannot know. This is the nice 'turning from the material,' the 'concentration,' the 'adoration,' the 'self-abstraction,' and similar devil's nonsense."[69] For Luther and his followers, *sola scriptura*, or "Scripture alone," was to be instead the test of what's true in one's life and in the life of the church. This approach was, of course, more threatening than all the mystics of Catholicism combined.

William Tyndale, another Protestant reformer, in England, was also then teaching that every person with a Bible—and he was busily, illegally, trying to supply them with those Bibles—should be learning for themselves what God wants for their lives. It is surprising, even in the twenty-first century, how often this attitude—that each person with a Bible understands easily and clearly what the Bible means—seeps into Catholic understanding and practice.

To discern God's will, there are rules and guidelines one must follow carefully, according to the *Exercises*, including questions to ask oneself to discern the spirits correctly and know what God intends. It is easy to see how the Exercises themselves, as they encourage each person who undergoes them with sincerity to see and feel themselves with Christ, and listen for his voice, were threatening to some. Tyndale began publishing his vernacular Bibles in 1525. Ignatius was encouraging people to understand God through the Exercises at that time, too.

Faber, with his tendency toward depression, would learn that all human life is full of experiences of desolation, of loss, of feeling distant from God, and sometimes these feelings come indeed from God, and sometimes they come from the world—those "enemies of our human nature." Ignatius was there as Faber's spiritual director to help him discern the one from the other. As he continued to discern God's will, the question was, to what would Faber devote himself?

## Spiritual and Religious Reform

The monastic orders were battered, just then, compared to the reputation they'd enjoyed a few hundred years earlier. There had been a time, for instance, when the abbot of Cluny, in the north of France, was second only to the pope in religious authority and power in Western Christendom. In the first half of the eleventh century, the great Odilo, abbot of Cluny, routinely received vast acreages of land grants for Masses to be perpetually said for the faithfully departed. This is how Cluny came to nearly rival the Papal States in territory held. Monks still worked at their trades, secure within the walls of their often-rich monasteries. And monks' prayers, coveted and precious, became more specialized as choir monks ruled the finest monasteries.

Those glory days had faded from view by the early sixteenth century. Friars—including Francis of Assisi's Franciscans, Dominic de Guzmán's Dominicans—for three centuries had moved monastic spirituality and practice out of the cloister and choir into town. A friar was a reformer of monastic ways, vowing poverty, chastity, and obedience, but not stability. Friars were itinerant and focused on preaching repentance and forgiveness to people on the streets and in university towns. Essential sacraments like the Holy Eucharist and confession were no longer confined behind tall walls. From their beginnings, friars of the mendicant orders worked with a pastoral strategy that was designed to adapt to social changes.

The power and security of monasteries, once so appealing, began to be seen more conspicuously as wealth, and that wealth looked unseemly and hoarded. Erasmus in his wicked satires, best sellers throughout Europe, called monks lax, worldly, and wasteful. And across the English Channel, in 1534, as soon as King Henry VIII was declared by Parliament the Supreme Head of the Church in England, he began to forcibly dissolve their monasteries, taking monastic estates and property as a reclaiming of assets on behalf of the people of England. Monks were described as an impediment to forward-looking faith. It was also a way to further stick a finger in the pope's eye.

Martin Luther had, of course, started his Reformation while still an Augustinian friar.

Among friars who remained committed Catholics, there were also evangelical religious fervor and desire for reform. The Capuchins had their start in 1520, just before Ignatius, Xavier, and Faber met in Paris, when a Franciscan, Matteo Bassi, began telling his spiritual brothers and superiors that God wanted him to be more faithful to the extreme poverty, simplicity, and solitude of St. Francis's original Rule. Matteo's superiors didn't respond kindly to the criticism and sought to silence him. This led Matteo to flee his friary in northern Italy—in the Marches, a region long home to fervent and passionate followers of Francis—and go into hiding among the Camaldolese monastic communities. It was while Matteo was hiding among Camaldolese monks that he adopted a way of dress and a habit of growing a beard that soon became trademarks of the Order of Friars Minor Capuchin. *Capuchin* is from the Italian *cappuccio*, or "hood," a simple head covering, often detached from the friar's cowl or habit. Beards and hoods became defining characteristics of these most austere Franciscans that Faber would occasionally meet on the roads and in cities. He met them less often, however, than Conventual or Observant Franciscans, because Capuchins were often hermits.

The Capuchins began to restore to Franciscanism its mendicancy, extreme poverty, and simplicity in every respect: manners, lifestyle, and living only for that day. They became highly recognizable. First, they wore no shoes. Second, their tunics and hoods were to be of the simplest, roughest available fabric, which was in those days a certain color of brown for which the cappuccino would later take its name. Many memorable Capuchin characters stand out from those days but most of all the third vicar-general of the province, Bernardino Ochino, who began preaching sermons that called not so much for personal reformation as for reformation within the church. When he was eventually summoned in 1543 by the pope to answer for his preaching, knowing that he'd be tried and probably convicted of heresy, he fled over the mountains to Switzerland to join John Calvin in Geneva.

## Seeking Truth and Abandoning Cooperation

Most reformers, including Catholics, as well as the new Protestant churches, believed they were the "true church" and, correspondingly, that all others were untrue. Appeals to religious or theological purity were not new, of course; they went back centuries to early church controversies. And heretical movements were nothing new. Most of all, in the mountainous regions of Europe, ancient heresies were kept alive. In such places, those who held to dangerous opinions—often centering on views of Christ that diverged from the teachings of the church, or notions that the world we live in is unreal or controlled by evil forces, or practices of asceticism and notions of purity that were unnatural and not Christian—felt safe from the reaches of Rome and empire.

Luther told his followers that reforming churches were the only "true" ones. He called the Catholic Church a whore and declared that it was trapped in a new sort of "Babylonian Captivity," having lost its way. John Calvin taught his followers something similar and set out to create a theocracy in Geneva that would enlist the state to help the church guide souls through their earthly sojourn and then safely to salvation and the afterlife. This was an era that knew nothing of the separation of church and state. On the contrary, each state was headed by a monarchy, and that monarchy believed its power derived directly from God—as per various lines in the Bible used to confirm such a perspective.

One more detail: There was another common belief that added more kindling to these fires. Namely, human beings have a holy obligation to correct one another when they have lost their way in matters of religious truth. This can be traced back to Thomas Aquinas, who taught in his *Summa Theologica* that it was worse to lose one's earthly life than to die in apostasy and lose eternal life.[70] Such an idea—embraced by the church—led logically to inquisitions. In Calvin's theocratic Geneva, for instance, the reformer himself would infamously oversee a burning at the stake of at least one deemed heretic (Michael Servetus, in 1553). And a few years after that, the second-generation Jesuit Robert Bellarmine (now *St.* Robert Bellarmine) would argue that Catholics in a Catholic state were not only entitled to but also responsible for executing heretics if that's what it took to conform them to Catholic ways of belief and practice.

Every opposing side affirmed its right and obligation to defend itself against those groups and states they believed heretical and to aid those who agreed with them in such states to overthrow their government and even kill a monarch. Monarchs may receive their right to reign from God, but that right is voided when that monarch is not found within the "true" church. This was when Christians did not believe that tolerance of religious differences was in their creed. Voltaire would write: "We have Jews in Bordeaux, Metz and Alsace; we also have Lutherans, Molinists and Jansenists. Could we not tolerate and accommodate Calvinists . . .? The more sects there are, the less dangerous each one of them becomes. Their sheer number makes each one of them weaker."[71] But that was a perspective of a later age.

A spirit of religious cooperation, absent in the embattled early sixteenth century, was present not only at the birth of democracy but also much earlier: the Caesars of ancient Rome understood this principle. At the time of the birth of Christ, many religions were tolerated in the Roman Empire. Caesars understood that spreading out the numbers was a way of keeping any one group from becoming too powerful. Emperor Constantine, after uniting east and west in the ancient Roman Empire, declared in the early fourth century: "Let those who still delight in error be made welcome to the same degree of peace and tranquility that those who believe have. For it may be that the restoration of equal privileges to all will prevail to lead them into the straight path. Let no one molest another, but let everyone do as his soul desires."[72] But for more than 1,500 years, religious tolerance was abandoned in most of the world. Even when Voltaire wrote the words quoted above, it was the 1760s, and he was pleading with his fellow Frenchmen to agree, since tortures and executions of Protestants were still taking place.

## The Spirit of Faber

At no point does it appear that Faber, either before or after discovering his vocation as a priest, had an appetite for politics or leadership on a corporate level. He must have surveyed his times with an eye of deep concern—and a lack of interest in joining the fights.

There were many competing ways of understanding the activity and intentions of God. What soon became the Society of Jesus was then in its nascent form. Other religious orders were focusing on preaching and catechesis; Jesuits would soon do that, as well, but in the short term, Faber realized that his passion was for showing people how to understand the working of their minds and emotions. How to discern the spirits. Through self-examination and imagination, he was learning to unravel what prevented him from surrendering to God and how to be truly present with God in daily life. He wanted to show others how to do that too.

He said his first Mass on the feast of St. Mary Magdalene, "my advocate and the advocate of all sinners, men and women," he wrote in his journal. He also recorded his gratitude for God's raising his soul "to so high a state" and for granting him the grace to see and care for things that have to do with God only rather than matters of worldly power, desire, or competitive advantage.[73]

In the memorable phrase of one of Faber's other friends, one of the other original Jesuits, Jerónimo Nadal, a member of the Society of Jesus was to become someone *simul in actione contemplativus* (simultaneously contemplative and active).[74] This was the case for Faber. This is what he was undergoing at Ignatius's direction. Faber was moving from his time of "first fervor," the naïveté of his early conversion, when everything seemed ideal and beautiful, toward the fullness of who he would become when the real challenges set in.

# 12

## They Are Companions of Jesus

*Pure naturalness and truth, in whatever age, still find*
*their time and their place.*[75]

—Michel de Montaigne

### Autumn 1534

The Kingdom of France changed during the early morning hours of October 18, 1534. Up until that day, the Protestant Reformation had been held at bay and didn't bother the most Catholic of countries. But on this early morning, dozens and perhaps hundreds of would-be Protestants plotted to change the course of history. They set out in the darkness in a coordinated campaign to spread propaganda in the form of leaflets and posters all over Paris and other major cities. *L'Affaire des Placards*, or the Affair of the Placards, the event is sometimes called in the annals of French history. The placards displayed Protestant slogans and sarcastic jabs at Catholicism.

There even appeared a poster on the door to the bedchamber of King Francis I, and that little bit of rebellion and heresy was too much for the normally tolerant-leaning king to bear. Most of the posters had been printed in Switzerland, and the campaign was a well-coordinated effort arranged by two Protestant pastors, one of whom, William Farel, had been educated at the University of Paris in the decade before Faber. Farel then taught philosophy for a while at the Collège du Cardinal-Lemoine. What had begun for him and others as Catholic humanism, nurtured by reform-minded bishops, had gradually turned into evangelical Protestantism, in part because of the expanding influence and encouragement of John Calvin in Geneva.

The crimes of October 18 in Paris, Tours, Rouen, and elsewhere were regarded by the king and the French parliament as a deadly serious instance of *lèse-majesté*, a crime against the monarchy, or treason. The instigators would be punished. So would those, including children, who did the actual pinning of the posters in their places. About three dozen culprits were soon identified and located. They were not students; nevertheless, the students of Faber's college and other colleges were required to be present for the torture and burnings at the stake that took place over the winter months that followed. Such an experience was seared into Faber's memory for the rest of his life. He would rarely speak of heretics in his memoirs, and when he used that word, both there and in his letters, he was always conciliatory.

## The Name of Jesus

We don't know for certain where the founding members of the Society of Jesus were on October 18 when L'Affaire des Placards took place. The spiritual brothers had returned from the experience on Montmartre with fervor and plans but without the intentions one might easily project onto them. John W. O'Malley, SJ, in his history of the Jesuits, explains that their intention to live in chastity and Christian commitment was paramount. But "despite these vows and the decision regarding ordination, they all insisted in later accounts of this crucial turning point in their lives that they had no intention of founding a new religious order."[76] The next six years would put them on a course to greater organization and formalized commitment, before Pope Paul III formally approved them as a new religious order by papal bull.

Since their time as students in Paris, these brothers had been united in purpose. As Faber writes: "We became one in desire and will and one in a firm resolve to take up that life we lead today—we, the present or future members of this Society."[77] By 1534, seven others had joined the original three roommates. Ignatius remained the group's inspiration, Xavier was their other best recruiter (a true extrovert), and Faber was a quiet, prayerful, and steady leader. Joining those three were, from youngest to oldest:

- **Paschase Broet,** French, nine years younger than Ignatius and six years Peter's senior

- **Claude Jay,** also from the Savoy, like Peter, and two years his senior. They reunited at university, having first known each other in school as boys in Thônes. Peter introduced Claude to the Exercises.
- **Jean Codure,** from Provence, two years younger than Peter. The only among the original group to predecease Peter (five years earlier, at the young age of thirty-three).
- **Simão Rodrigues,** Portuguese nobleman, a benefactor of King John III of Portugal even before he arrived at the University of Paris. He would later cause scandal for the Jesuits.
- **Nicolás Bobadilla,** Castilian, five years younger than Peter but lived a lifetime longer. He was a hothead but instrumental in the growth of the order. Bobadilla died in 1590 at the age of seventy-nine.
- **Diego Laìnez,** also Castilian, met Ignatius in Paris outside the university. He was later with Faber on the way to the Council of Trent and became the second superior general of the order.
- **Alfonso Salmerón,** Laìnez's friend, was from Toledo, Spain. He, too, met Ignatius in Paris outside the university. He would become a person of theological renown and travel all over Europe from Scotland to Naples, where he helped found the first Jesuit college.

There were other young men, as well, whom these early companions attempted to interest in Ignatius's ideas and Exercises, as well as various other pieties and even a pilgrimage to Jerusalem. All these things interested the original three intensely.

Each man was a Christian with an intellectual approach to faith, the sort of approach that characterizes the discussions one participates in and relishes at university. Without a call to preaching, like the Dominicans and Franciscans, who ran many of the universities, these friends of Ignatius were what Justin Martyr called "philosophers." One of Justin Martyr's statements, deemed ponderous by some then and now, made perfect sense to this group of religiously committed men: "The majority of the philosophers have simply neglected to inquire . . . whether or not a divine providence takes care of us, as if this knowledge were unnecessary to our happiness."[78]

They began to call themselves the Company of Jesus, or the Companions of Jesus. What more natural and obvious description could they have imagined? They were, of course, Jesus' companions. They intended to "walk" and "journey" with him in the way that saints and would-be saints had tried to follow the Gospel for centuries. So, what later became the Society of Jesus began as a fraternity of men who were spiritual companions and who were together, simply, the Companions, or friends, of Jesus.

Still, the name could come to sound presumptuous to some—particularly when this casual cohort of companions became an order. All the original ten could do was remind people that they did not set out to be more than what they had begun quite simply in commitment to one another.

One of the fellow students who was not there that day on Montmartre, Jerónimo Nadal, would become a prominent Jesuit Companion years later. But while a student in Paris with Ignatius, Peter, and the others, he rejected their overtures. Jerónimo was uninterested in their spirituality and pieties. Interestingly, it was even years after he became a priest and a doctor of theology in Avignon that Nadal underwent a spiritual conversion in the mid-1540s while in his native Majorca. It was then that he remembered the old "Company of Jesus" and went to Rome, looking to join them there.[79]

## Reviving Personal Piety

Relationships were cordial between universities across Europe and Oxford and Cambridge in England. It wasn't until 1536 that King Henry VIII suppressed the study of canon law and Scholastic philosophy, after his split with Rome. Students also traveled freely from Paris to Bologna to Cracow to Naples to Mainz, and "university culture" became a draw not only for young men interested in ideas, in cities, and in preparing for lives in court, medicine, law, and church; university cities became engulfed with other people too. There were servants, tailors, sporting instructors, riding masters, horse grooms, theater managers, men (and women) who worked in houses of entertainment, who surrounded a university, offering their services and their wares. The result was excitement and energy unlike anything in the country. Universities built the cities of Europe centuries before the Industrial Revolution would do the same.

But the society of the original ten was consciously living in the tradition of St. Benedict's Rule and St. Francis of Assisi's charisma. They were reformers more than theologians, but they had much in common with both. They believed in a crusade against what keeps ordinary people from following the Christ who died, was resurrected, and redeems. The result was that Ignatius's cohort was able to create a religious intellectual movement that began to look a lot like a religious order of the Catholic Church. Ignatius had a gift for showing "the intellectual how he could become a child of God, a saint—*with* all his gifts and values of mind, grace, personality." And "the Jesuits showed the astonished and eager intelligentsia of Europe how the intellectual could become blessed and holy, through constant accomplishment in his calling as historian, astronomer, jurist, mathematician, nobleman, soldier or politician. . . . It was suddenly possible to develop all one's personal forces in religious service."[80]

This was an era when popular spirituality was being reborn. Yes, Christian mystics such as Origen in Egypt in the third century and Bernard of Clairvaux in twelfth-century France had linked imagination with divine revelation. They had taught that revelation was a holy gift to those prepared to receive it. But when mystics like these then wrote from their imaginative visions, it was mostly inaccessible to everyday people. They wrote for other mystics, theologians, prelates, and monks. What was comprehensible to the few excluded the many. Then there was the subject matter of these theological, saintly writings: it was abstruse and metaphysical, rarely practical and applicable.

However, briefly, in the early thirteenth century with the birth of Franciscanism, this situation had changed. Francis of Assisi set out to create simple, vernacular praises of God and to reconnect ordinary Christians with the created world through verse and song and ritual. It was Francis who also innovated in personal spirituality by creating tangible pieties such as the stations of the cross and the Nativity crèche. But his influence had waned by the start of the sixteenth century.

Ignatius sought to change that situation in the church. Ordinary people—not just those who wanted to make vows to be Companions of Jesus—were urged to use their imaginations to place themselves beside Christ and to understand themselves as contemporaries with Jesus. This is what the *Spiritual Exercises* taught as the "composition of place." They were instructed in the daily Examen. They were reminded to go to confession, to go to Mass. Faber and Ignatius and the others were not only practicing pieties themselves; they also believed that spiritual practices such as these were what would truly reform the lives of Christians and churches.

They stood in a quiet line of tradition that included women such as Catherine of Siena in Italy (see her *Dialogues*) and Julian of Norwich in England (see her *Revelations*), who offered to everyday people wisdom about prayer and connection with God. There were also occasionally friars and priests who would guide their directees using iconography to relive as participants the events of Christ's life on the earth. There was, for instance, a popular book of meditations on the life of Christ, once attributed to the early Franciscan Bonaventure, that was a best seller in the late Middle Ages. We know of its best-seller status because of the large number of manuscript copies that have been found, in many languages. A representative example from this book is the scene of Christ journeying to his baptism, which is accompanied by text that includes this passage:

> He started on the road from Nazareth toward Jerusalem to the Jordan where John was baptizing, which place was eighteen miles from Jerusalem. Alone He walks, the Lord of the world, for He does not yet have disciples. Observe Him therefore diligently for the sake of God as He goes alone, barefoot, on such a long journey, and have deep compassion for Him. "What should we think, O Lord, of your going? Are you not above all the kings of the earth? O Lord of lords, where are the barons and counts, the dukes and cavaliers, the horses and camels, the elephants, the wagon and train with beautiful and rich harness, and the multitude of companions?"[81]

This part of the book, with question after question like this, goes on for another full page. These are among the tools that the first Jesuits, good students of Christian spirituality, were offering in new ways through the Spiritual Exercises.

In Paris today, the eighteenth arrondissement, on the Right Bank of the river Seine, is known for several things. Most of all, people know it as one of the still-vibrant cabaret sections of the city, home to the refurbished Moulin Rouge as well as many other establishments near Métro station Blanche. Second most known among the eighteenth arrondissement's attractions are the buildings that were once the homes and studios of great nineteenth- and early-twentieth-century Parisian painters, including Monet, Renoir, Toulouse-Lautrec, and Pissarro. Vincent Van Gogh also spent time there. As *Rough Guides* or Rick Steves would advise, visitors to Paris today should get off the Métro at stations Anvers or Pigalle to see this part of the city, also known for a hill upon which sits a church, and the hill is known as Montmartre.

Although less than five hundred feet high, Montmartre is the highest point in Paris. In Faber's time, Montmartre was an independent village with wineries and windmills. Situated on top of this *mont* today is a minor basilica constructed in the late nineteenth century and eventually consecrated during the First World War, called Sacré-Coeur. More important and much older is the Church of Saint Peter of Montmartre. In 1534, it went by a different name.

On August 15, 1534, Ignatius of Loyola, Francis Xavier, Peter Faber, and four others—Bobadilla, Laìnez, Rodrigues, and Salmerón—traveled across Paris to the Martyrium of Saint Denis on Montmartre to formally mark their intention to found a religious order and make a pilgrimage to Jerusalem. The original founder of a church on this site was the third-century St. Denis, bishop of Paris. By 1534 it was a functioning abbey but also an active place of pilgrimage. There in the crypt of the Martyrium (the word means a small church, architecturally circular, octagonal, or cruciform, centered around remains of a holy martyr), where the bones of St. Denis are revered, the "Company of Jesus," as they then called themselves, pronounced the traditional vows of poverty and chastity. This is known to history as the "Vow of Montmartre."

If you visit Paris today looking for the Martyrium of St. Denis, significant in the history of the Jesuit order and the life of Peter Faber, you won't find it. This is one of the many ways in which the search for the newest saint of the Society of Jesus is easily hampered. The place where Faber and the others stood that day was smashed to pieces by the marauding crowds of the French Revolution. It was tentatively rebuilt a century later under the direction of a female religious order.

The vows that the seven made that day centered on one vow in particular that was a medieval preoccupation, an inheritance from the not-yet-closed age of crusading: they would travel as pilgrims to Palestine and, whether there or back in Europe, would consider themselves in service to the pope and the church. The ritual of the occasion was performed by Faber, still the only priest of the group. He consecrated and gave them all the sacrament of communion. The Society of Jesus was born.

# PART TWO

# 13

# Models of Leadership

*Ignatius would become primarily an administrator. . . . Xavier became*
*the globe-trotting missionary. . . . Favre, on the other hand, spent the rest*
*of his life as a spiritual counselor sent to spread the Catholic faith*
*during the Reformation.*[82]

—James Martin, SJ

## 1535–1538

Ignatius's health remained fragile, and his Companions of Jesus began urging him to take care of himself by returning home to Spain. It's interesting that the notion of a weeks-long journey on foot and horseback on war-torn and dangerous byways was thought to be wise for an ailing man, but the possibility of complete respite upon arrival must have been convincing. Ignatius left in April 1535, telling his friends that Faber was their new, if temporary, spiritual head. This period of nascent leadership of what was a nascent band of brothers ended up lasting six months.

It was a tempestuous time for any Christian leader. Christianity itself had just entered a period of intense humiliation.[83] Every major institution of the Catholic Church, and by extension, of Western civilization itself, was in a crisis of meaning. Every foundation was being questioned. To be Christian had been a given of nearly every society, large or small, a century earlier, but now there was dispute over what that even meant. Before, its meaning was simply implicit. Even worse, the churches and the institutions that fed them and were fed by them were tagged with the label of corruption. In real terms, Christianity was in ruins.

Ignatius—and this demonstrates how time was understood in longer and more patient terms—declared his intentions to be gone for two years. They would all meet, he said, God willing, in Venice in the spring of 1537. From there they would sail together for the Levant, finally. Imagine how such a reunion would take place in those days, without the ease of modern transportation and communication. Letters were delivered in weeks or months, and journeys were made on foot or on horseback, taking several weeks to go a distance that today might be achieved in a single morning. Like a massive ocean liner that requires many miles of distance to come to a stop in open water, Ignatius and the others would somehow, sometime, meet up again in Venice in two years' time.

## To Venice, Attempting to Reach Zion

Charles V of Spain and Francis I of France were threatening each other's lands and pride, each preparing to go to war, as the young cohort of Jesus enthusiasts were beginning to prepare for their journey to the Holy Land. Not far from the Latin Quarter of Paris, where they all lived, was the church already famous throughout Christendom, Sainte-Chapelle ("Holy Chapel"), where King Louis IX had housed cartloads of relics of the Holy Passion of Christ that two Dominican friars carried back from a war-torn Levant on his behalf. Louis bought them from the emperor of Constantinople, which is also where the friars picked them up. All this took place precisely three centuries before Peter and the others were devising their own plan to visit the again-besieged holy places where Christ suffered and died. The young would-be pilgrims surely visited Sainte-Chapelle frequently, honoring Christ's crown of thorns and the other items there for the benefit of a penitent Christian's prayers.

The cohort decided to cut short the theological studies that several of them hadn't yet completed and to leave early for Venice. They left just before winter was about to begin. "On November 15, 1536, we set out from Paris together," Faber recounts.[84]

While they were traveling from Paris to Venice, Pope Paul III, less than two years Roman pontiff, was forming a commission of reform-minded cardinals of the church to investigate some of the charges made popular by people like Luther and Melanchthon. What substance was there to the charges of financial improprieties relating to indulgences and simony, for instance? The report, *Consilium de Emendanda Ecclesias*, was given to Paul III the following spring. It was clear that reforms were indeed necessary, even according to Roman cardinals and Curia insiders. Despite the report's being confidential, a copy was smuggled out of Rome and, by 1538, published by Luther himself in vernacular German, complete with his own commentary in the margins.

Some of the cardinals and Curia members who proposed reforms to the Holy Father in *Consilium de Emendanda Ecclesias* went on to form a movement known as the *Spirituali*. This included Cardinals Gasparo Contarini and Reginald Pole, and Vittoria Colonna, a woman poet, artist, and friend of Michelangelo. All three had been gracious and generous to the first companions of the Society of Jesus since the days when they left Venice and before they ended up in Rome. An intense missional, evangelistic spirit was shared between them. It is credited to the influence of Cardinal Contarini that Pope Paul III approved the Society of Jesus in its earliest stages; Contarini also underwent the process of the *Spiritual Exercises* at this time, most likely under the spiritual direction of Ignatius himself.[85]

The history of the first Jesuits could be written entirely around accounts of their long journeys. This one from Paris to Venice covered about eight hundred miles, in sloppy winter, through cities, plains, and mountains, through northern Italy and Bavaria. It took them two months, traveling throughout Advent and Christmas.

They had basic provisions and pocket money. Their vow of poverty was unlike the mendicancy of those reforming Franciscans, the Capuchins. Faber and the others were not begging for their bread. But the journey was made no less difficult or dangerous by having the most basic of provisions. They would endure storms and snows, and they would encounter men with weapons at the ready along the way. It was a time of war. When was it not?

And if the history of the early Jesuits could be written around their travels, the history of Peter Faber could be written, as he often framed it himself in his memoirs, around the opportunities travel provided for him to meet people influenced by the Protestant Reformation: "We traveled on foot, passing through Lorraine and Germany where there were already many Lutheran or Zwinglian towns," he remembers six years after this early journey. It is just like him to be in mind of such details. The Martin Luther behind Lutheranism is well known; "Zwinglian" refers to the followers of Ulrich Zwingli, who, as a pastor at the age of thirty-five, in 1519 began preaching in Zurich criticisms of the Catholic Church similar to those of Luther in nearby Germany. Zwingli's influence was felt in many parishes throughout Switzerland. He died in battle, fighting to defend Zurich, which he'd turned into a theocracy, only five years before the journey of Faber and the others from Paris to Venice. There was danger from the Zwinglians, as well as from those whom they might meet along the way. As one historian has put it: "Despite their precautions to take a longer route, they nevertheless ran into French soldiers, who demanded that they identify themselves. The Spaniards in the group demurely kept their silence while the Frenchmen spoke up for all: 'We are students of Paris.'"[86]

Upon arrival in Venice in January 1537, all nine fervent men took up residence in two Venetian hospitals to care for the sick and dying. A major trading center, Venice was also one of the richest and largest cities in Europe, and its medical care was probably the best in the world. Nevertheless, *hospital* in the early sixteenth century was a term used in much the same way we use *hospice* today. Plague was a constant threat, and parish priests were even required by law to track who was ill in their parish and from what sort of ailment. Those deemed seriously ill, or likely to be incurable, were sent to hospital. There were also crude surgeries performed with regularity, similar to those experienced by Ignatius in Spain to fix his wounds from the battlefield. A hospital was a place that had inmates more than patients. A hospital was where people went to die.

In a letter, Ignatius says that they were in the hospitals in Venice "in order to care for the sick who are in poverty, doing the jobs that are most demeaning and physically repugnant."[87] This would include cleaning sores, changing bedpans, and perhaps assisting physicians when they had to perform certain procedures that passed then as preventive treatments. And, just as priests were often the ones diagnosing illnesses, physicians were often involved in seeing that the administration of the sacrament to the dying took place. For this reason, for instance, beginning in 1555, Jews were forbidden from being members of the Venetian College of Physicians; they could practice only in the Jewish Ghetto.[88]

In the spring of 1537, during Lent, the companions traveled back to Rome on a pilgrimage of penitence and obtained an audience with Pope Paul III. Not only was the pope present but also some of his cardinals and advisers. A rigorous questioning took place, but the companions came out of it well. Ignatius recalls in a letter written a couple months later: "The upshot was that the Pope was very pleased with them, as were all those present at the discussion."[89] He puts it that way because Ignatius himself was absent that day—he was afraid that some among the pope's number might remember that Ignatius had been accused of heresy not long before in Paris.

It would be more than two years before Paul III would give his formal permission for the creation of a religious order, but on this first occasion, the companions sought two things from him. First, they wanted a papal blessing to travel to Palestine, not as simple pilgrims, for pilgrims do not commonly have an audience with the pope, but as ministers. That permission was granted. Their second request was granted, as well: They all sought ordination to the priesthood. Their work was to be priestly work. Paul III saw in the men a desire to live in poverty and faithfulness to the church, and he saw no reason they should not be able to return to the Patriarchate of Venice, with his blessing, and see any bishop there, asking to be ordained. They did so. And then came the waiting.

When people would ask them who they were, or what religious group or order they were attached to, they began to respond that they were of no group but the Company of Jesus, who was their only religious superior.[90] This would have had them sounding at times suspiciously like some of the Protestant reformers who were then consistently in the public eye and worldly news, if it weren't for the early companions' accompanying outspoken devotion to the commands of the Roman pontiff.

The situation in Palestine was violently out of hand at that time. Since 1516, when the Ottoman Turks reconquered the Holy Land from Christian occupiers and made it part of the Ottoman Empire, the land had been in Ottoman Muslim hands. The Ottomans controlled all the Middle East and were then at the height of their military, political, and economic power. Their recent conquests reached even into parts of Europe such as the city of Belgrade and the Greek island of Rhodes in the eastern Mediterranean, which was, before being conquered by the Turks, the headquarters of the Knights Hospitaller, the medieval Catholic religious order that existed precisely to serve and keep safe pilgrims coming from and going to the Holy Land. (In his memoir, Ignatius mentions how, before taking his first trip to the Holy Land in 1523, the capture of Rhodes in December 1522 was the primary reason for most pilgrims, giving up hope of visiting.)

Then, in 1537, precisely when the early Jesuits wanted to travel to Zion to walk where Jesus had walked, the tenth sultan of the Ottoman Empire, Suleiman I—Suleiman the Magnificent, as he was known in the West—was in the middle of a massive rebuilding project to fortify the walls of Jerusalem. There were no Westerners, and almost no Christians of any kind, visiting the Holy Land then. Palestine would remain under Ottoman control for centuries, until the end of the First World War.

The companions, including Faber, were meanwhile spending the summer of 1537 in solitude and prayer and practicing corporal works of mercy. They had dispersed throughout the Papal States of northern Italy in groups of two or three. Those who were as yet not ordained sought to become so, and they all sought to study, pray, and wait for the right time to travel. Two were near Padua, two in Trieste, two in Bassano del Grappa, two in Verona. Faber was, with Ignatius and Diego Laìnez, back in Venice. There they spent the summer while they sought a ship that could carry them to Antioch or the Nile Delta. But there wouldn't be a suitable one. They tried again for a ship in early 1538, but again none could be found.

## Preaching in Rome

The new order really came into its own in the year 1538—not in Jerusalem, where the men had longed to go, and not in Venice, far from Pope Paul III and his Curia. In Rome. It all began with a controversy.

Faber had begun teaching theology at the University of Rome the previous November, immediately after arriving from Vicenza. He and the others, who slowly arrived in the Eternal City early in the new year, were summoned by the pope and granted permission to hear confessions, distribute the Holy Sacrament, and preach throughout the Roman diocese. Such preaching was carefully controlled in those days when reformers and pseudo-reformers were frequently threatening to take their issues to the seat of the church and when the memory of dramatic cases such as Friar Girolamo Savonarola, OP—who was excommunicated and burned at the stake in 1498 for refusing to stop preaching in Florence upon orders of the pope—was still fresh. Besides, many thought that preaching was the mark of these new Protestants; since the reformers had made preaching their hallmark, Catholics had tended to shy from it, even though the world's largest religious order, the Franciscans, was founded as a preaching order.

Faber and the others preached all over the papal city, much to the astonishment of everyday Romans who were used to hearing preaching only during the penitential seasons of Advent and Lent and rarely outside Rome's primary churches. This is what Jesus did in the Gospels—but it was also what Protestants were doing throughout Europe, particularly because they were often unwelcome in the churches of a city where they were attempting to evangelize. So, people wondered who these new preachers of poverty, repentance, and faithfulness to the Catholic Church were. Were they genuine? Whose side were they on?

What's more, the preaching of the Companions of Jesus was often intense. Sermons could last for hours—so long, in fact, that sometimes a companion would offer to his listeners (and probably relish for himself) an actual intermission.[91] Then, in addition to the preaching, their hearing of confessions caused many more—this time, the clergy and members of the Curia—to grumble. The companions had been granted permission to hear confessions not only from men but from women as well, and this led to speculations. It seems that the Society of Jesus was spending too much time encouraging confessions from Rome's large prostitute population.

## Accusations of Impropriety

The Curia still didn't know fully what to make of such earnest men. Fervor among religious was something to be wary of. Society members were accused of a variety of possible improprieties related to their work in Rome's seedier neighborhoods. Ignatius, Faber, and the others were greatly pained at this, so sincere were they in their devotion to their duties and so ardent was their desire to please the pope. So, Ignatius insisted on an official inquiry into the charges. There was no other way, he believed, to fully clear their names. The inquiry took place in the early autumn of 1538 under the auspices of the governor of Rome, who then "put his name to a document vindicating the life and teaching of Ignatius and his companions."[92]

Then came a resolution that was to be stamped upon the Society of Jesus as its most defining characteristic for centuries. Faber states it almost like a rule of life:

> We offered ourselves as a complete sacrifice to our sovereign Pope Paul III, for him to decide how we might best serve Christ and do good for all who submit to the authority of the Apostolic See, while we lived in poverty, readying ourselves to set off for the Indies, should the pontiff will it.[93]

John W. O'Malley, SJ, one of the most important Jesuit historians of our own time, has explained this special vow most helpfully:

> They formulated for themselves a special "fourth" vow that obliged them to travel anywhere in the world where there was hope of God's greater service and the good of souls—a vow often misunderstood as a kind of loyalty oath to the Pope, whereas it is really a vow to be a missionary. Even as the Order was receiving papal approval in 1540, St. Francis Xavier was on his way to India, thence to Japan, and almost to China before he died in 1552. The missionary impulse would continue to define the Order down to the present.[94]

Faber goes on to praise God that he and the others were deemed able to serve the universal church in this way, having heard the will of Jesus Christ through the voice of Paul III, making it clear they were to serve both church and pope for the rest of their lives.

# 14

## Crisscrossing the Continent

*Magellan had a well-painted globe in which the entire world was depicted.*
*And on it he indicated the route he proposed to take.*[95]
—Bartolomé de Las Casas

### May 1539–Summer 1542

Christopher Columbus and Ferdinand Magellan knew the world wasn't flat. Every educated person knew, before the turn of the sixteenth century, that "to the ends of the earth" was a metaphor. They knew that there was no falling off a precipice, and yet one had to begin to see the world for oneself to grasp what going to the ends of the earth really meant. Like Columbus and Magellan, who were also devout Catholics, the first Jesuits saw a big world in front of them.

"In the entire universe the earth is the substance of our glory and our only habitation. Here it is that we wield our power and covet wealth, throw humankind into an uproar, and launch wars, even civil ones," wrote Pliny the Elder fifteen centuries earlier, perhaps having no idea how true his words would remain.[96] The world was then, as now, the only place to fight over for power and influence. Even where there is belief in heaven and fear of judgment, it seems there isn't so much of it to keep men from doing awful things to one another, and the Spanish and Portuguese kingdoms were exploring the world at the same time the Jesuit order was being born.

Among the first Jesuits, Faber was not the most predisposed by nature or inclination to encounter a contentious world head-on. He was probably the gentlest and most retiring of the original cohort, yet he was also a man of obedience and had just enough of the explorer in him to follow his superiors' orders and requests with a spirit of adventure. To Faber, Pope Paul III was not only Christ's vicar on earth; the pope's voice and his orders on behalf of Christ and church were "the clearest of calls."[97] Faber's devotion and commitment to the papal office were unambiguous. This is interesting, because Paul III was known to have fathered children with mistresses and to have been one of the more notoriously nepotistic of popes in memory. Faber's personal scruples may have been overwhelmed by his sense of duty and respect for divine authority. From the spring of 1539 until the end of his short life, Faber would follow the pope's instructions, which were usually relayed to him second- or thirdhand.

"At the bidding of the Roman pontiff . . ." is how Faber usually realizes what he is being instructed to do next. This is how he often records what happens next in his life, in the *Memoriale*. Such bidding is often communicated to Faber through Ignatius, the most visible member of the cohort, its elder founder, and its widely recognized leader. It was Ignatius who famously instructed his brothers to go out into the world and set it aflame, but it was also Ignatius who told Faber and others always to go where there was the most need.

Faber, Xavier, Ignatius, Diego Laìnez, and the others had been together for years by early 1539. They had formed a wandering fraternity and referred to themselves freely as the Companions of Jesus. It was as if they couldn't imagine a more apt name. They already had sore feet, having walked back and forth many times across the Papal States, wearing out their sandals. They had earned master's degrees in theology in Paris, which became, after their devotion to the Roman pontiff, the second most common perception of their charism: they were well educated. After their studies, they'd also become adept in corporal works of mercy, in preaching, hearing confessions, and of course, directing the spiritually curious in the Exercises.

No one taught, explained, and guided the Exercises as Faber did, Ignatius used to say. No one took them to his heart the way Peter did, and no one had his ability to understand the needs of others so well. For this reason, much of Faber's time in the years to come would be spent leading prelates, monks, princes, and priests to experience Christ through the Exercises.

In May 1539, the pope requested that two among Ignatius's number go with a cardinal of the church to Parma. They were to instruct and exhort people with inspiring defenses of the Catholic faith. Faber and fellow priest Diego Laìnez left on this, their first apostolic mission, to help counter growing heresy in the Papal States of northern Italy, a region the companions knew well from their time in Venice.

It is with unusual warmth that Faber alludes in his diary to an incident in which one of his old pals from Paris came to see him in Parma. Jerónimo Doménech was a Spaniard like Ignatius and Xavier, and they'd all known one another at the University of Paris. Back in Spain after school, on his own, Jerónimo worked toward ordination and became a priest. He then wanted to rekindle his old friendships, as well as see what sort of work the Ignatius group was doing on behalf of the Holy See. Jerónimo's uncle, however, felt differently. He wanted his ward to pursue a career that he had in mind for him. Becoming a wandering priest reformer—which is what the Companions of Jesus were then known as—was not exactly a career, let alone a well-defined religious path. "I will remember what took place in Sissa!"[98] Faber writes in his diary, remembering with a smile the time when he helped his friend by sending Jerónimo to Sissa at precisely the time when his angry uncle was arriving in Parma to confront his nephew.

Later in the same passage, Faber shows another bit of humor. "Remember that illness of yours!" he says, speaking this time to himself with fondness and delight at another memory from those days. How many people remember illness fondly? "You can't forget the great spiritual profit you derived from that!" Faber writes to himself.

The work in Parma went very well. A few months later, in a September letter from Faber to Ignatius, written by Faber as he's preparing to wrap up in Parma, he shows us how progress was being measured. Faber reports the "harvest" he is seeing gathered. As they'd done in Venice, Faber made the hospital in Parma his center of activities, and he reported that people were arriving, sometimes daily, for confession and communion. He was seeing many laypeople, including women, and encouraging priests in town to accept "the excellent practice" of hearing confessions more frequently, in fact, whenever someone came asking for the sacrament. He also reported that priests had learned to give the Exercises to their parishioners. They were teaching the Ten Commandments and the seven deadly sins to laypeople in ways that made understanding this most basic catechesis fresh. Faber reported to Ignatius that many priests had been "brought back to a good life" through the Exercises and that their preaching had benefited from this too, in ways difficult to measure but easy to witness firsthand. Again, Faber emphasized in this early letter that people, both clergy and lay, were being "moved to a good life."[99]

The interior life was growing for Faber, too. One imagines Faber and Ignatius with notebook and pen in hand while doing the Exercises and making their own confessions, recording spiritual perceptions and experiences as a scientist records observable data. The Jesuits were not the first group to find their own desiring important, and they certainly were not the first to take the imagination seriously, but they were perhaps first to make desire and imagination so central to Christian piety. Their personal reflections—beginning like simple jottings in notebooks—were records of images that came to them, notes of desires that consumed them, which then passed, replaced by others. Their examinations of conscience proceeded similarly, creatively but also methodically. These were all exercises of the spirit, as they understood it. Faber would soon begin teaching this pedagogy of the heart to the famous and powerful throughout Europe.

Along with his vow of obedience, Faber knew what God wanted from him through his regular prayer life, as guided by Ignatius. This is the practice of every Jesuit. Where should he go next? What should he do once he's there? There is, for a member of the Society of Jesus, an assumption that imagination comes from a place inside that is attuned to divine realities. Identification with Jesus Christ is at the heart of the life. This is exemplified in practicing what Ignatius referred to as three degrees of humility. The first degree is to love Jesus Christ so much as to identify with him fully. You will follow Christ, your love, anywhere necessary. The second degree of humility focuses less on the person of Jesus and more on his message. You seek to love and dedicate yourself to the Gospel, to the message of the Beatitudes, to the redemptive vision of Christ for the world. The third degree of humility is to identify with Christ in *his* humility—even in his rejection, humiliation, and passion. To undergo this yourself, both imaginatively through prayer and in real-world experience, is to be prepared to choose what Jesus chose wherever you are in your own life.

Those are specific exercises that Faber underwent. In those exercises, as in others, a Jesuit endeavors to see, hear, smell, and touch what Jesus saw, heard, smelled, and touched. It is important not to put those sensing words in quote marks, which would cause the reader to read them as "so-called" or "supposedly." In Faber's prayer life, there was little sense of remove from Jesus' experience when prayer was done right.

A Jesuit does what Jesus tells him to do—even to the point, in Shusaku Endo's novel *Silence*, when a Jesuit priest apostasies by stepping on an image of Christ to save the lives of others being threatened with death, because he hears a voice say, "Trample on me!" This fictional example (recently made into a film by Martin Scorsese) is understood by Jesuits as an authentic representation of how one hears God in Ignatian spirituality. Faber used to record taking concerns to the Lord in prayer and receiving answers that spoke to him "interiorly." How does a Jesuit believe that he knows God's message for him? It isn't necessarily that one hears God's voice audibly in the eardrum, but there is a voice of prayer—and when it comes, it is a result of a very real encounter.

# 15

# Protestants, Protestants Everywhere!

*If you study the sixteenth century, you are inevitably present at something
like the aftermath of a particularly disastrous car-crash. All around are
half-demolished structures, debris, people figuring out how to make sense of
lives that have suddenly been transformed.*[100]
—Diarmaid MacCulloch

The breakdown of Christendom was already underway when the Augustinian
friar Martin Luther became a worldwide celebrity, or an infamous heretic
(opinions varied widely), for his denouncements of Roman Catholic religious
practice. In the context of our twenty-first-century ecumenism, we lose sight
of all that was feared lost by those whom Luther was battering. For example,
on the recent five hundredth anniversary of the nailing of the Ninety-Five
Theses in Wittenberg, a popular Jesuit spiritual magazine published a special
issue titled "The Reformation: A Gift from God?"[101] This was clearly not the
view held by any of the members of the Society of Jesus during the decades of
Luther's Protestant revolt.

What happened next from the side of the institutional Catholic Church is
called the Counter-Reformation, also known as the Catholic Reformation or
Catholic Renewal. No matter what you call it, the Society of Jesus was at its
center. In fact, Faber and his Jesuit brothers were sometimes confused with
Protestant reformers because both the Jesuits and the Protestants were stirring
up the emotions of people and asking them to consider truer and holier inspirations in their lives. The primary difference was the Jesuit vow to obey the
Roman pontiff.

Luther's supporters were numerous in his native Germany, where German princes quickly took his side for a fight against Rome. But Italy and France, too, had their share of people predisposed to listen to him. The entire Holy Roman Empire was in upheaval, and the lands long dominated by popes and the Curia were nevertheless (or not surprisingly) peopled with Catholics who were less sincerely Christian than, say, the Catholics in faraway Spain. Two thousand kilometers away from Rome, Spain, at the other end of Christendom, was the real hotbed of loyalty to the pope and his Church. Spain was far away from Bohemia, where much of the firestorm first began with the nascent Protestant reformers, one century earlier. It was in Bohemia in 1415 that a Catholic priest and theologian named Jan Hus was burned at the stake. Equally distant from the center of Catholicism was the English Catholic John Wycliffe, whose vernacular translations of Scripture were banned throughout Europe. The church would have burned Wycliffe, too, if it had caught up with him before he died of natural causes. As it was, it condemned his life and work posthumously, exhumed his ashes from consecrated ground, and burned them.

Among Faber's contemporaries, there was Michael Diller, born around 1500 and graduated from the University of Wittenberg in 1523. A professed Augustinian monk like Luther, Diller became prior of the Augustinian monastery in Speyer, a German town already becoming radicalized by the Reformation. While there, Diller learned from Luther's polemics and soon took up the cause of "justification by faith," arguing against the meaning and purpose of indulgences. Diller was also an evangelical in the mold of Luther and so did not place obedience to his superiors and his vows above spreading what he believed to be the Gospel.

There was also Martin Bucer, Faber's contemporary and friend, who started his adult life as a Dominican friar. It was after meeting Luther that Bucer was convinced to renounce his vows and become a Protestant preacher in France. We will meet Bucer again in the next chapter. He and Faber were often together at colloquies aimed at bringing Protestants and Catholics back together, and Bucer believed he could sway Catholics to his cause as much as Faber believed that he could pastorally show Protestants the way back home.

## Chiseling Away at the Edifice

The effect of all this activity was a weakened Holy See and Rome. Fearing for the future of the Papal States, Pope Clement VII aligned himself with France, Venice, and Milan, causing the Catholic Holy Roman Emperor Charles V to call the pope a "wolf"—rather than a "shepherd"—to his flock and then defy him by sacking Rome in 1527. Charles V even took Pope Clement prisoner in Castel Sant'Angelo for six months. Meanwhile, in England King Henry VIII wanted the pope to annul his marriage to Catherine of Aragon, Charles V's aunt. That never happened, leading to the English Reformation. Back in Rome, a victorious Charles V began to consider "the Lutheran question," listening to the complaints of German princes regarding the Church that he otherwise loved. Three years later, in 1530, a weak and subservient Pope Clement emerged and even crowned Charles V in Bologna.

Those who wanted to mediate and reconcile in the conflict over reformations were working against a stream of negative sentiment once Pope Clement VII died. As one historian puts it, "The rift with Protestantism and the shock left by the devastation of Rome bred a sterner spirit in the Church and Papacy. . . . [M]en of ruthless will and unbending morality sat on the throne of Saint Peter, marshaling and leading the resurgent forces of Catholicism."[102] Pope Paul III, elected in October 1534, became a friend to the Society of Jesus—but he was also the candidate who was picked for his strength and ability to fight.

For his part, Luther was a man who harbored hatred easily. In 1538, he was still preaching that the Catholic Church and its clergy, religious, and cardinals worshipped the pope rather than Christ. He reserved no hope or interest in reconciliation. Two years later, he designed and published a fake coat of arms for the Holy See that portended the sort of violence that many pastors and princes dreaded. His description of this faux display tells its story: Luther said that the pope "banned me and burnt me and stuck me in the behind of the Devil, so I will hang him on his own keys."[103] Luther was a hothead who, after leaving the church, was without any real counselors or superiors to curb his more negative qualities.

Faber felt that the growing schism was caused by a lack of love and understanding, by Christians standing as opponents rather than brothers. He wanted to befriend Luther and Melanchthon but was ultimately forbidden to do so by the Holy See, to whom each individual member of the Companions of Jesus looked in those days. In other words, Faber believed that the Protestant Reformation might have been avoided with pastoral care. His attitude was quite different from that of the pope and of most every other leader in the church. With characteristic gentleness and empathy, Faber was passionately concerned about men like Bucer and Calvin, with whom he shared a language, and even Martin Luther, Melanchthon, and Henry VIII (who was becoming a real reformer in his own right).

One day in January 1545, toward the end of his life, Faber paused to reflect on Luther and his rebellion. Luther was then sixty-one, constantly fighting physical ailments and growing short tempered, even making anti-Semitic statements in his writings and sermons. His wife—he had married a nun—is famously reported to have said to him then, "Husband, you are too rude." But Faber couldn't call him a heretic. It seems he couldn't bring himself to do that. The closest he comes is to refer to Luther—and other famous men who were Protestant reformers, including Henry VIII—as "those who are in manifest danger of damnation." Even then, Faber writes in his memoir of feeling "affected by a feeling of deep compassion."[104]

Faber rarely uses the word *heretic* in his memoirs, and when he does so in his letters, he's usually deploring how heretics are being summarily handled, refusing to consider them a type of person at all. Typically for Faber, restoration of those in heresy remained his determination, hope, and intention. "We need to win their goodwill," he wrote in another letter from March 1546 to fellow Jesuit Diego Laìnez, "so that they will love us and accord us a good place in their hearts."[105] That is a shockingly sympathetic way for any devout Catholic priest of that decade to speak of Protestant reformers. A few years earlier, Faber reflected in *Memoriale* that God most of all dislikes the ways that heretics are trying to reform the church. When they speak the truth, they too often are speaking it without "the spirit of truth."[106] Like Pope Francis, who in the twenty-first century has shocked the world by refusing to condemn people in situations that seem to easily call for condemnation, Faber refuses to do this to prominent Protestants everywhere.

Also like Pope Francis in the twenty-first century, Faber in the sixteenth quickly turned to point the finger at himself. In that entry in his memoirs from January 1545, immediately after writing of his deep compassion for Luther and the others, who might possibly be in trouble regarding eternity, Peter writes that "something . . . could [also] easily be taken as a condemnation of myself and of others like me." In every instance, Faber explains to himself and anyone else who might later read his words: God gives us time to repent our wrongs and to find a more complete conversion by the gift of grace.

His friend Ignatius sometimes took a slightly less conciliatory approach. He better understood Luther's taste for fighting, and his passions were also easily inflamed as were the German's. (And for his part in this play of personalities, Luther had no sweet, sensitive, receptive confidant and friend to compare to Ignatius's Peter Faber.)

The late twentieth-century Jesuit philosopher Michel de Certeau once said, "The mysticism of the sixteenth and seventeenth centuries proliferated in proximity to a loss." In other words, feelings of absence tend to multiply feelings of desire.[107] It isn't difficult to follow the threads to see the sort of unraveled world that Faber was living in. One only has to imagine what he had witnessed in his lifetime—the religious turmoil, the preacher-inspired violence, and the use of empire to enforce what was meant to be heavenly—to understand what every sincere Christian was struggling to hold on to in those times.

But before this moment came to a close, and hope was dashed for bringing this church back together, both Pope Paul III and Charles V sensed that Faber might be helpful.

# 16

## Worms and Diets

*[They faced] a pastoral obligation of the highest urgency.*[108]
—John W. O'Malley

### 1539–1541

Faber took a spirit of gentleness and conciliation with him throughout his travels. He was not a missionary in the way that Francis Xavier was. They were both sent again and again on missions—Xavier to more exotic, foreign lands; Faber within more familiar, continental Europe—and it is no accident that Faber rarely approached the people he'd traveled to see as if he had what they desperately needed. That wasn't his missionary approach. He seems instead to have seen his job, most of all, as listening. Such gifts usually pass by quietly, are rarely remarked upon. By contrast, Xavier's gifts were more visible and remarkable. There was a letter of Ignatius's, for instance, to King Ferdinand I of the Romans, bragging (or simply accounting?) that Francis Xavier had recently in a single year "converted 80,000 people."[109] The nature of Xavier's work in India and the Far East was also different from what Faber was pursuing in Europe.

Faber would spend the next two years participating in formal dialogue sessions with Protestant reformers at the request of the pope, his spiritual brothers, and sometimes Emperor Charles V. Wearing his cassock, carrying his staff, with missal and breviary in a shoulder bag, he went from Portugal to Spain to Germany (twice), across Switzerland, and throughout Italy.

In October 1540, Faber was asked to accompany Dr. Pedro Ortiz, a lay theologian and professor from the University of Paris, to Spain—until Charles V intervened, sending an emissary to find the men en route, redirecting them to Worms, Germany, where the Colloquy of Worms was soon to begin. This was one of the emperor's attempts to reconcile Catholics and Protestants in Germany and, by extension, throughout his empire. John Eck was there in Worms to represent the Catholic side. Eck had been publishing, lecturing, and debating against Luther and Lutheran ideas since 1519. Luther's good friend Philipp Melanchthon was also in Worms, representing the Protestants. The forecast couldn't have been very clear for agreement. They seem to have agreed with Catholics only on the doctrine of original sin.

The Colloquy of Worms was Faber's first experience of the sort of dialogue that takes place at gatherings of people standing ideologically and theologically opposed to one another. The emperor hoped Faber might find common ground between the sides, but he didn't. They didn't. And Faber went away convinced that only personal relationships could make a real difference, change an opinion, or influence for good.

As became common for him, Faber was occupied with more than his formal work while in Worms with Ortiz, who was known to be a firebrand. Surely, the two men found little to unite them beyond Catholic doctrine. While writing letters home to Ignatius about how poorly the colloquy was proceeding, Faber was receiving from Christ special care in the form of a new devotional practice. He reminds himself in *Memoriale*, "You were to take up and practice [this] until your death." This practice was an addition to Faber's usual praying of the daily breviary by remembering moments in the lives of Christ and Our Lady. While the disappointments of the colloquy were all around him, Faber believed his Lord was gifting him with "special consolations."[110]

When the Colloquy of Worms came to an inglorious end on January 14, 1541, Pope Paul III next sent Faber to the Diet of Regensburg, also in Germany. There, Emperor Charles V would again preside, seeking any possible Catholic-Protestant reconciliation. Everyone who watched Faber there saw that he was not the usual papal representative. Sent to uphold the teachings of the church against Protestant challenges, Peter avoided theological debate entirely. He was interested most of all in friendship, worship, and pastoral work. He had no interest in, and distrusted, political maneuvering and the preponderance of opinion.

Also, ever the mystic, traveling from Worms to Regensburg, Faber was actively recording in his *Memoriale*: "When I passed through mountains, fields, or vineyards, many methods of prayer occurred to me." He looked at fields awaiting the sun of spring (it was February) and gave thanks for what he saw as abundance. He appealed to the local saints, angels, and archangels of the places through which he traveled to guard and protect him and to intercede on behalf of himself and those with whom he had dialogue. This was his primary work. He remained passionately concerned about Protestant leaders and the growing schism, but again Faber was disappointed in the process and outcome at the Diet of Regensburg.

While in that city, we see clearly Faber the pastor. He records "remarkable things" that "our Lord granted me grace to accomplish."[111] These were, namely, confessions of noblemen and noblewomen of the imperial court—people of influence. As a result, Faber is certain that "much seed was sown for the still greater good." He also tells his journal that many of these same important people, of Spanish, Italian, and Germany distinction, made the Spiritual Exercises under his own direction. And he discovered Gertrude of Eisleben's *Life and Revelations* for the first time, a book that would deeply influence his own life of prayer. (The woman who became St. Gertrude in 1677 was only just being discovered in Faber's early sixteenth century.)

Before leaving Regensburg, on July 9, 1541, Peter also reconfirmed his vows of chastity, poverty, and obedience—to both the pope and his friend Ignatius, whom the Companions of Jesus had elected as their first general. He mailed this in a letter to Ignatius in Rome.

From this moment on, it seems that Faber is on one long journey. Throughout, he shows himself to be kind, respectful, and, most of all, nonthreatening. Leaving Regensburg, he and Ortiz and some others left the Bavarian city, traveling up the Danube toward Switzerland. They crossed the mountains and stayed for a few days in Faber's home region of the Savoy. "We passed through my native district," Peter tells us, and then into France proper where they were arrested, mostly for being a group primarily of Spaniards. It was surely Faber and not Ortiz who conciliated in that situation! This is an instance, in fact, that demonstrates Faber's personal gifts in ways that are deeply human, without a tinge of hagiography. He easily made fast friends with their captors. Faber even records that the captain of the armory that had taken them captive soon "sought confession and confessed to me." They all parted as friends.[112]

Faber carried Gertrude of Eisleben's assurances of Christ's love with him thereafter wherever he went. In her *Life and Revelations*, Gertrude's message revolves around personal statements such as the following:

> O Sacred Heart of Jesus, fountain of eternal life, Your Heart is a glowing furnace of Love. You are my refuge and my sanctuary.
>
> Lord, you have granted me your secret friendship by opening the sacred ark of your divinity, your deified heart, to me in so many ways as to be the source of all my happiness; sometimes imparting it freely, sometimes as a special mark of our mutual friendship. (various editions, chapter xxii)

These were a mystic's words of faith, despite all surroundings.

It was then, in prayer, that Peter received from his Lord a deep desire to remember the following eight people of importance and to pray earnestly for them. He records these names in his journal. He says that Christ asked him to pray for these people "without taking notice of their faults." He names them:

The Supreme Pontiff *(Pope Paul III)*
The Emperor *(Charles V)*
The King of France *(Francis I)*
The King of England *(Henry VIII)*
Martin Luther
The Grand Turk *(this is how Peter refers to Suleiman I, also known as Suleiman the Magnificent, the reigning sultan of the Ottoman Empire)*
Martin Bucer *(Protestant reformer)*
Philipp Melanchthon *(with whom he'd just been in Worms and Regensburg)*

Too many people were judging these men, Faber reflects, resolving instead to show each the "holy compassion" and "good spirit" of his prayers.[113] Then, he continued with Ortiz toward Spain.

## Hither and Yon

Just as he had prayed to St. Sebald while passing through Nuremberg and St. Maximin while in Trier, Germany, it was while passing through the regions and cities of Spain that Faber prayed to St. Narcissus in Gerona and St. Eulalia in Barcelona. One can almost track the trajectory of their journey west by the saints Faber invokes for aid. "Help me by [your] prayers to produce some good fruit," he remembers praying frequently to the cloud of witnesses.[114] He drew a direct line of connection between his activities in a place and the prayers of the saints in that place.

He wasn't in Spain with Ortiz for long, because one of the cardinals of the church wrote on behalf of the pope for Faber to return to Germany. It was in Germany that he was most needed. Return Faber did, on many of the roads he'd just traversed, back to Speyer. While on the road, he remembers that Christ gave him feelings of love and hope for the welfare of seven special cities that were particularly embattled for Christians at that time. Again, he names them in a list of intentions:

> Wittenberg *(the capital of Lutheranism)*
> Kiev *(although Faber calls it "the capital of Sarmatia," an antiquated term for Russia-Poland)*
> Geneva *(home to Calvin's theocracy)*
> Constantinople
> Antioch *(in the Holy Land, then under Muslim control)*
> Jerusalem
> Alexandria *(also in Muslim territory)*

The idealist wanted one day to be able to say Mass in each of these places.[115]

Back in Speyer, he was soon directing clergy and others in the Spiritual Exercises, saying Masses, giving spiritual counseling, supervising Jesuit novices, and preaching on obedience and prayer. He remained in Germany for a year and was often upset that Catholic spiritual practices such as prayers and feasts of the saints were not being observed as they once had been. As chronicled in his journal, he was continually revisiting the passion of Christ, the works of God in Scripture, and the saints and feasts of the church, finding fresh meaning in them. His practice was to say Mass and then walk home through crowded neighborhoods, taking close and prayerful notice of the people on the busy streets. At one point, in July of that year, he laments to his journal the sorrow he felt when reflecting that other Christians didn't seem to meditate as he did or reflect deeply enough on the mysteries of Christ's life and passion. This causes him to redouble his efforts to teach and be an example to those for whom he is responsible.[116]

He came up with a special way to pray each evening, making the sign of the cross and repeating certain sentences from the office of compline:

> "Keep wicked dreams far from us."
> "May the all-powerful Lord grant us a peaceful night and a
>     perfect end."
> The Our Father.
> The Hail Mary.
> The Nicene Creed.

His new intention was to add this cycle of prayers at the end of every evening, before sleep, after his usual litanies and daily Examen.[117] His life was increasingly full of pieties.

Even when the desire for piety left him, as it sometimes did, Faber took time to contemplate the purpose for this spiritual dryness. Sadness, bitterness, depression, weakness, wandering—these are terms he uses to describe himself at times. But then he concluded it was God's intention for him to undergo periods of days or weeks of spiritual dissatisfaction so as to keep always fresh and new "the desire of finding devotion." This will probably strike the twenty-first-century reader as both remarkably wise and psychologically modern! God didn't want Faber to become too satisfied or habitual in his piety, Faber figured.[118]

He continued to talk with the angels and saints associated with each town or place as he entered or passed by it. He said he was always looking for ways to offer blessings for what he saw along the way—good crops, a healthy river, friendly people. For expressions of praise, Faber coined the phrase "deed or action words," saying that they are the best sort of speech. This gentleness of speech expressed itself in how Peter dealt with strangers. At a time when travel on roads and byways was considered highly dangerous, particularly for those unaccompanied by knights or other men with arms, Faber writes that, "seeing strangers on the road, even if they are soldiers or other men, we should not allow ourselves to have any suspicions against them. Our thought should be that they are good people, and we should pray for their good and should in a way unite ourselves to them with a bond of charity and love. Thus we will rid ourselves of fear, rash judgments, and the like."[119]

He continued to remember the patron saint for each day. (He'd learned them as a child, and they stuck in his memory like glue.) These very real men and women were his daily companions. He'd appeal to them "to obtain for us not only virtues and salvation for our spirits but in particular whatever can strengthen, heal, and preserve the body and each of its parts." They gave him courage to enter dangerous places and speak with individuals he feared, more than once.

Peter set out to be as active as he could, which was always his tendency. He spent long periods of time with two chaplains who were personally assigned to Princesses Maria and Juana, daughters of Empress Isabella of Portugal and Charles V, the king of Spain and Holy Roman Emperor. Faber led the chaplains through the Spiritual Exercises. The chaplains could then better guide the princesses, even if there were no Jesuits around. Faber was also making plans to meet with two bishops and a doctor of canon law, who all wanted to begin the Exercises under Peter's direction.

It seems that some in the church in Germany were associating Faber and the Jesuits with Protestants because both groups were, at that time, stirring up passions among people. Faber and other Jesuits were, like the Protestants, counseling people "in terms of reformation and changing their lives." It must have been difficult to discern who was who in those days. Faber took all of this in stride, telling Ignatius that he even rejoiced in being assigned such faults and singling out the devotion and faith he was witnessing in the clergy in Speyer as particularly praiseworthy.[120]

After a few weeks, Faber seemed to realize how God was moving him, and so he set out to meet Protestants and reformers. He had come to see first-hand that their disappointments with the church were founded on realities. Everyone could see that simony—the purchase of positions of authority and spiritual favors—was rampant. Religious illiteracy and insincerity among the clergy were all too common. There was immorality, often sexual immorality, among senior church leaders. All of this was wrong. And for many years, Martin Luther's followers had been allowed to gather and worship in this freethinking, freedom-loving town. Faber set out to meet them, as well as to find ordinary Catholics—hat makers, cobblers, butchers, tanners, and sailors—anxious to learn the lessons of the Spiritual Exercises. His pastoral heart was full.

He was teaching people that the value of an indulgence lies exactly in what it promises, but it does not work magically or transactionally. "Our souls should be prepared," he taught, "by a total turning away from every sin."[121] And the worst thing he could say about Luther was to refer to "that idle faith" the Protestants teach—a reference to Luther's principle of *sola fides*, or "faith alone," as what leads to salvation, without good works.[122] Faber also believed that most of the Protestant leaders were like children who forsook their mothers in order to behave and believe whatever they wished.[123]

It was six weeks after his initial disappointment upon arriving in Speyer, on June 15, 1542, that Faber set to recording in writing some of the graces he had received from God. If it weren't for that book, we would know very little about him. Although he doesn't refer to the day on which he began the writing by the Gregorian calendar—he may, in fact, have been unaware of that date (most people usually were)—it was "the octave day of the Body of Christ" when, as

Peter puts it, "there came to me a strong desire." He'd long wanted to record what God "had given me."[124]

Faber had been instructed by the pope early that year, 1542, to travel to Speyer to assist a cardinal who was the papal nuncio of Germany, but by the time Faber arrived in April, the cardinal had moved on to visit other cities, leaving instructions for Peter to do whatever work he felt God calling him to do. There followed a brief period of uncertainty, when Faber wrote to Ignatius expressing the "great longing" he had to receive letters from him, "so that I can learn what I ought to do," he says. Faber was worried that he'd made some mistakes in his holy obedience, as he must have arrived later than was advisable, after the cardinal had departed Germany. "The truth is that he leaves me much freedom," Faber writes to Ignatius, "but without any sense of delight."[125]

Faber writes of his desire "to begin writing down so as to remember them some of the spiritual things which the Lord has given me from his hand in prayer: whether as counsel about the course to take, or for contemplation or understanding, or for action." This was, and would become, a deeply Jesuit way of spiritual understanding: a charting of the soul's progress.

The result, the *Memoriale*, is a lost classic of Christian spiritual literature. In English, it fills 250 pages with a rare sort of wisdom. It has been compared to Augustine's *Confessions*, but only because both books take an introspective look at past sins and failures and look to God for present guidance. Both men also speak personally, in the first person. But the spirits of Augustine and Peter couldn't be more different. Peter doesn't wrestle with ideas or seek to chronicle his changes of mind as Augustine earnestly does. *Memoriale* is more accurately compared to Brother Lawrence's *Practice of the Presence of God*: practical, honest, revealing, innocently humble. Like Brother Lawrence, who prayed while washing the kitchen pots and pans, Faber thanks God in simple things, just as he became adept at finding God in the complexities of life. His spiritual autobiography—which of course we've been sampling since the moment this book began—tells us relatively little about Faber's day-to-day movements. It is mostly about his private inner life. Peter wanted to record these things for his own edification.

He had much time in Speyer—too much, perhaps—to explore his own good and bad spirits. But by September 1542, the cardinal of Mainz sent for him to come consult on theological matters related to Protestant-Catholic orthodoxy, and Faber did. Then he returned to Speyer. But the cardinal appreciated his work and wrote again, saying, come join in the work in Mainz. This was to Faber's disappointment because he had made many friends in Speyer and was hesitant to leave. So hesitant was Peter to leave Speyer, in fact, that he would confide to his journal, "I made up my mind to obey the command of the very reverend archbishop-elector."[126] There were times when his vow of obedience made difficult decisions easy.

Thus began his long journey to the Council of Trent.

# 17

## Interlude: "Blessed be the upsetter of hearts."

"Desire what is essential and original," Faber writes in *Memoriale*.[127] This sentence gets at the psychological brilliance of the Exercises and how they specifically transformed Peter's life.

Faber discovers that desires are good, not bad, and that finding what's essential in the heart comes only when we find God there. As Pope Francis said in his homily about him on January 3, 2014, "Faber could discern God's voice in his desires." Finding God's will is possible when we accept that God has a unique plan—an identity, purpose, and destiny—that's ours alone.

Every person who attempts to follow Christ with faithfulness feels desolation, loneliness, anger, and other upsetting emotions throughout the average day. To deny these and put on a happy face is to miss the purpose of emotions entirely.

When there is a knot in your stomach from nervousness, God is close by. We see this beautifully in this passage that Faber writes in a letter to a king: "Blessed be the upsetter of hearts." Precisely when you cannot see the right way to go, God is present. Stop and look carefully. And in your joy as well as your sadness, God is there. God is in our turmoil and our desires. These are not the simple, pious messages of a man seeking private peace. A truly spiritual life doesn't aim at that. Rather, it aims at holiness before God and with one's neighbors.

# 18

# Overcoming Demons and the Dark

*The glory of God is a human being fully alive. The glory of a human being is the beholding of God.*
—St. Irenaeus

## 1543

The cardinal of Mainz who sent for Faber was none other than Albert of Brandenburg, whom we first met in chapter 2. This was the Albert who paid for his red hat by hiring John Tetzel to sell indulgences. In the intervening decades, Albert had lost none of his distaste for Protestants and none of his tone deafness when it came to the need for reform. As archbishop in Mainz, he had recently taken to adding gold, relics, and art to his churches more extravagantly than ever before, employing the Latin motto *Domine, dilexi decorem domus tuae*: "Lord, I love the adornment of your house."

Faber had to struggle more than ever with discerning spirits, both in himself and in others for whom he served as spiritual director. Inside him was a contrary spirit that disagreed with his good spirit and the Spirit of God. Sometimes this contrary spirit was also regarded as a "wicked angel," as it were, whispering in his ear what is untrue: future misfortunes, imaginary trials, fears and worries, depression and hopelessness, exaggerations of the negative, the faults of others. These were all found in that bad spirit that is never inspired by God but desires us to listen to falsity. This evil spirit "is not only evil but a liar as well," says Faber.[128]

It was in this interior battle that he was sometimes occupied, especially after arriving in Mainz. He found himself questioning his undertakings, even his very apostolate. What was the purpose in it all? He had to sturdy himself with daily attention in prayer and by conversation with his fellow Jesuits to be sure he was consistently an instrument of that good spirit, not the bad. Evidence of success would then follow naturally: feelings of hopefulness, desire for God, joy in prayer, fresh energy to show charity to one's neighbor. "We must earnestly ask the Holy Spirit to bring under control all the spirits that dwell in us," he wrote in his journal a year later.[129]

Still, the bad spirits were returning often.

When Ignatius had first introduced Peter to the Spiritual Exercises, he'd warned him of their dangers. Chief among these was the responsibility one had to accept upon entering the desires of the spirit, what the Society of Jesus refers to as the "discernment of spirits." Beginning with Ignatius, every Jesuit has been taught to discern spirits: to learn to know which voices to heed and which to dispel from one's mind and heart. One model for this discernment is the voice that Jesus heard in the Garden of Gethsemane. Jesus does not have an audible conversation with the Father, nor are the words of the Father recorded by the Gospel writers. But a real conversation takes place, nonetheless.

Discernment of spirits is essential to what one learns in the First and Second Weeks of the Exercises, and for a man whose friends knew he was already prone to bouts of depression, these were risky times for Faber. He was afflicted, and not in any supernatural way, with periods of inexplicable sadness, doubt, emptiness, and worry. He was simply a sensitive soul. It wasn't uncommon, Peter himself tells us, for these periods of low spirits to last for three days, by which time "the grace of God would effectively put an end to it."[130] At one point, in late October 1542 in Mainz, he felt particularly low. He tells his journal how he begged God to elevate his mind by grace, and his language is all about desperately seeking "growth" and "looking upwards" rather than the opposite tendencies to which he was feeling disposed.[131]

As time went on in Mainz and Faber battled the bad spirits that often plagued him, he slowly began to mount their obstacles and reach higher places. Just before Christmas in 1542, he wrote in his *Memories* of a difference he was experiencing in his preaching. He was more clearly communicating, and his points were made more coherently. He says that his memory, too, was improving. The sense of being untroubled by disruptive spirits made a difference in every aspect of his life. (Just as quickly, of course, Faber then reminds himself in the journal of his wickedness, his unworthiness, ultimate shamefulness, and need for grace!)[132]

Despite all this interior attention, his pastoral approach to the Reformation continued. In fact, his intense self-examination and response to the tumult in the church were intimately linked. Faber could never shake the notion that the calamities in the world, particularly the wars and conflicts brought on by religious differences, were somehow, in part, the result of "the accumulated sins of many men"—not least of all, himself.[133]

That Christmas Day, while saying Mass in one of the great churches of Mainz, he would have surprised many people present had he been speaking in the vernacular, rather than saying the Mass and preaching in the customary Latin—for his intentions that day were focused on the importance not only of "rooting out heresies" in Germany but also of finding "peace among Christian princes," meaning Catholic and Protestant both. This is how he wrote it in his journal, and perhaps this is also how he described his feelings about the situation in Mainz to friends and colleagues during those days.[134]

## Albert's Castle

Two months after settling in Mainz, Peter walked a two days' journey to Aschaffenburg on the River Main to visit the castle of Cardinal Albert. What is now a town of sixty-two square kilometers in northwest Bavaria was then the seat and property of the archbishopric of Mainz. It was the season of Christmas, in 1542.

Albert's collection of relics and religious images was world class, and Faber was awed by them in two chapels reserved for the lord archbishop. They discussed plans for the future and the churchwide council the pope was wanting to convene in Trent. Pope Paul III had been talking of the need for this gathering for several years, and when the Diet of Regensburg failed to bring unity between the Catholic Church and what had become much more than a few Protestant preachers, the Council of Trent seemed one last necessary attempt for unity and consolidation. But the archbishop urged Faber to remain in Mainz, not to prepare to leave for Trent, which had been his earlier instruction.

It is interesting that Faber records struggling, just then, with the notion of seeking the approval of powerful men while in Aschaffenburg. There is no better way of remaining in God's goodwill than being forsaken of men, just as Christ was beaten and suffered at the hands of the powerful, he reflects in his journal: "The esteem of men should never be sought or, if offered, accepted unless it is intended for the benefit of one's fellowmen and not for itself."[135] It seems that Albert told Peter of his earnest feelings toward reform in the church, eliciting the Jesuit's help on those terms.

Faber remained with the lord archbishop on the River Main for two weeks.

## Getting into the Mind of the Other

While remaining in Aschaffenburg, Faber reflected on paper what it must be like to become a Protestant. For several pages, he writes a succession of reflections, and what he felt were realizations, of how one begins on the path to "abandoning" the church. Faber attempted to get into the mind and heart of the reformer, imagining with great psychological acumen what would take place. Perhaps it goes like this:

- Pieties and practices begin to be abandoned, because rational explanations for them cannot easily be found for them in their minds.
- They then begin to seek reasons for everything, including matters of faith.
- They forget that spiritual gifts are infused by the Holy Spirit and that true faith is Catholic and supernatural.
- Their faith begins to transform into something of their own making.
- By the time they begin to speak to others of their new views, they insist on a principle of not allowing passion to guide religious decisions.

"Then," he reflects, "they require [the person whom they are trying to turn from the Church] to seek out a faith for himself . . . by the Scripture and by reasoning, having recourse to no other arbiter than his own private judgment."

From all this, it is clear that by this point, Faber had begun to rehearse arguments in favor of Catholic faith and Catholic unity in ways he had earlier avoided. His conversations with Protestants had become numerous and wide reaching. Still, he concluded these pages reminding himself what he was then often reminding others:

> If you are confronted with someone who is sincerely unwilling or unable to be helped by you in these matters, don't argue with him. Don't even discuss. Fly from there, and pray for him.[136]

Faber then returned to Mainz, where he threw himself back into his German apostolate of caring for souls.

## Feelings of Dread in Germany

"Fiat! Fiat!" Faber writes over and over in his journal, after times of recording sadness, then returning to moments of renewed desire for God and decisions to redouble his pastoral efforts. The Latin expression translates as "Let it be done!"

He kept moving from place to place, following invitations and commitments to help those in need. Back in Mainz, he stayed with a parish priest who was preparing to become a Carthusian. This led Faber to find alternate rooms in a poor and unsafe part of the city and then record his feelings of gratitude for all the different lodgings he experienced. "As a life, it was wandering and restless," he records with a sort of wistfulness in March 1543, adding that God wanted his life that way.[137] From his idyllic childhood in the Savoy, to university apartments in the Latin Quarter of Paris, to filthy "hospitals" in Venice and elsewhere, to sleeping in the open air while traveling, and to occasional stays in the castles of princes and cardinals, Faber had seen much of life by his early forties.

He kept talking with Protestants in Germany and to those the reformers were attempting to influence. Faber urged them all to be careful about essential doctrines such as justification and sanctification and not to depart from a shared vocabulary: "If everyone goes about writing books with new terminology aimed to fit their ideas, we'll have only more and more sects, doctrines, and definitions. Not in sacred matters!"

That spring, while saying Mass on the Feast of the Holy Cross, he was in Mainz in the church that shared the name of that feast, reflecting on how sad it was that would-be reformers felt the need to damage and destroy sacred objects. In the Church of the Holy Cross at that time was a crucifix someone had rescued from the Rhine, and another had been discovered nearby with its head violently knocked off.[138] Germany's defections and divisions saddened him often, leaving him at times with a sense of dread for the future, imagining there could one day be a "total defection from the faith." Then, just as quickly, he scolds the bad spirit that gave him such a thought![139] And he wishes that the reformers could see the renewal going on in Catholic churches: people returning from Confession renewed in joy, the strength coming upon people after Communion, the fervency with which the clergy are celebrating Mass. Search everywhere, Faber told a Carthusian prior friend, for those who don't want reformation as much as they want to "tenaciously cling" to traditional faith.[140]

It was that same Carthusian prior who, in August 1543, invited Faber to visit Cologne to assist the charterhouse and other Catholic leaders in resisting the effects of Lutherans and other Protestants in their archdiocese. With the apparent blessing of a foolish cardinal-archbishop in Cologne, reformers such as Martin Bucer and Philipp Melanchthon had been coming and going, preaching in the churches, for a year already.[141] A plan for reformation in the church had even been drawn up, authored by the Protestants. Faber was to work there assiduously, but not for more than a month.

## Off to Portugal

In early September, Ignatius wrote from Rome, asking his old friend to leave for Portugal. John III, the Portuguese king, had asked the Jesuits for Peter by name. John III was in the middle of his thirty-five-year reign, undertaking some of his most adventurous and risky expansions of what had once been a tiny Iberian kingdom to India and China.

Faber was to represent the Holy See in the royal court in Lisbon, performing tasks that seem odd today for a significant religious leader. He was to be a private tutor and spiritual father to Princess Maria Manuela, the king's eldest daughter. Not being heir to the throne, Maria was engaged to be married to Philip II, the future king of Spain. Faber was to accompany Princess Maria from Lisbon to Salamanca for the ceremony.

Of course, these tasks were not Ignatius's only intentions for his friend at the other end of Europe. Faber's presence in Portugal and Spain might bring opportunities for recruiting new Jesuits and creating new Jesuit foundations.

However, it took him nearly a year to arrive in Lisbon. Travel wasn't that terribly slow in the sixteenth century; Faber was told in Antwerp that a ship wouldn't be available to him until late December, so he went to Louvain. Then, in January 1544, he received word that his plans for traveling to Portugal were altogether canceled, but he was to send twelve other Jesuits in his place. That he did, and then he returned to his post and relationships in Cologne. Faber was still enjoying the unpredictability of his life and its frequent travels when, five months later, in the middle of the summer of 1544, King John III called for him again by name. Peter writes, "I left the city on July 12 with seven heads from the holy bodies of the eleven thousand virgins" in tow.[142] He was taking holy relics with him for strength!

In the fall of 1544, finally arriving in Évora, in the central part of the Kingdom of Portugal, Faber spent his first weeks among the courtiers of King John III. He must have been listless, easily succumbing to his natural tendency toward diffidence, in such an environment, it being so contrary to what he knew and appreciated.

Before Christmas, with the king's approval he moved from Évora to Coimbra, 175 miles up the Atlantic Coast, where the Jesuit community was beginning to grow in a university town under the leadership of the twelve Jesuits Faber had sent in his stead the year before. In Coimbra, Faber continued to battle low spirits, bad spirits, and what at times he referred to as "stubborn resistance in my soul." These were again days of discerning spirits but also battling depression, centuries before we understood such ailments. He records in his *Memoriale* feelings of sadness despite what he knew should be the joyful season of Epiphany in January 1545.

There were other "demons" troubling Faber too. His spiritual brother—the fourth man to join the Society of Jesus, Simão Rodrigues—was in 1545 back in his native Portugal serving as leader, then as provincial, of the order. A charismatic man with strong emotion and intelligence, Rodrigues was several years younger than the other founding twelve. With great energy, he helped to increase the number of would-be Jesuits beyond expectations. Men were drawn to Rodrigues, and many were even quickly trained as missionaries and sent abroad, as the Jesuits were seeking to rapidly fulfill their mission as well as grow in numbers.

But Rodrigues was prone to the tendency of religious enthusiasm in ways that were harmful to discipline as well as to the Gospel. He welcomed novices who were probably not suited to the life, and he preached an excessive asceticism, quite literally taking it "to the streets," leading Dark Ages–type processions through the city center of Coimbra and other towns, declaring the need for all to confess, do penance, and publicly humiliate themselves with self-flagellation. In those public processions, Rodrigues was often at the lead, demonstrating a form of faith that left Faber uncomfortable.

When Ignatius got word of this practice, it caused a crisis of obedience in the order. Obedience to one another or in a chain of command was not something Ignatius had given much thought to. He and Faber and Xavier had been clear on their obedience to the Holy Father, but beyond that, the virtue and vow appeared to be opaque to some Jesuits abroad.

Eventually, Ignatius would summon Rodrigues to Rome. He wanted to stop what he regarded as these "proud humiliations." But most of all he wanted to make clear that obedience to one's superiors was essential for their order to function effectively and for God to be praised. In Rome, three fellow Jesuits served as judges at a religious tribunal, which quickly convicted a recalcitrant and unrepentant Rodrigues of disobedience and excess. For years, the province in Portugal—which was strategically important as a port and gateway for Jesuit missionaries leaving for the continents of Asia, Africa, and the Americas—was a troublesome one. Ignatius wrote letters to reinstruct them on the Jesuit charism, pointing out that other religious orders may excel at fasting and vigils and other forms of asceticism, but that was not the heart of what it means to be a member of the Society of Jesus. Most of all, Ignatius made clear, obedience is absolutely necessary for the chain of command:

> It is not because superiors happen to be very prudent, or very good people, nor because they are endowed with any other gifts of God Our Lord, that they are to be obeyed, but because they stand for Him and have His authority. . . . So no matter who your superiors are, I would like you all to practice recognizing in them Christ Our Lord.[143]

Rodrigues would not return until he became much older, somewhat gentler, and obedient once again to the wishes of his superiors.

Faber's gift for hearing confessions grew throughout this, his final year. As in other areas of his religious life, he showed how much compassion and humility he brought to this priestly task. In Coimbra, in early 1545, he was busy hearing the confessions of novices, many of them young Portuguese men with very little previous religious instruction or understanding and some of whom brought serious sins with them to the novitiate.

The first thing to do, Faber had advised a deacon one year earlier, whom he was urging to apply his talents to the hearing of confessions, is to ask the penitent if his last confession was complete and if every penance appointed by the last confessor had been performed. If so, Peter explained, the deacon could know that he had less to do than he would otherwise. The practicality is so obvious, and yet one rarely finds this sort of advice in the letters of other saints from this period. Most of all, Faber wanted to recruit this deacon for the spiritual work of hearing confessions—"helping souls," as Faber calls it.[144]

Always he was sweet and gentle—sometimes shockingly so for a priest of his era—and increasingly so, as he aged, which is also unusual. "In general, try to get the penitent to look into himself and state his own sins without fear and without any intimidation stemming from your words," he advised deacon Cornelius Wischaven, who would years later become an important Jesuit.[145] Throughout a multipage letter on how to hear confessions, Faber's advice revolves around how to listen, when to talk and when not to talk, spiritual needs that differ in people of different ages, and effective and ineffective ways of exhortation. He clearly took the confessor-penitent relationship to be a serious matter for both parties, and his goals for outcomes sound a whole lot like friendship. Confessors should not only "set the penitent straight" but not leave "until he has reached a proper frame of mind." A confessor isn't there only to make sure a penitent satisfies the requirements of penance for sins committed but also to do all he can to "improv[e] their lives in the future."[146]

That same year, writing to the Carthusians back in Cologne, Peter penned instructions that aimed to apply the teaching of the church to "what will chiefly help [anyone] in beginning his life anew." How does one do this? First, by making "a careful review" of one's "past life, year by year, and in bitterness of soul to make a general confession" of all past sins. Imagine how long this might take. This was not a conversion process for the weak willed or the easy-going. For this reason, Peter identified this and the other points in this letter as being "for an individual person's self-reformation."[147] The allusion was not accidental: the true reformation was what happens inside oneself. But a careful year-by-year review was likely not possible without some help. Peter advised making "use of an excellent physician and advisor"; he would help the one confessing to feel stronger in his remorse and to turn more determinedly away from sins and frailties, toward what is good and true.

This had become an essential aspect of his apostolate: showing people how to start over.

From Coimbra, Faber returned to Évora, and after a few more weeks there, he left with a young theologian, Jesuit Antonio Araoz, who would eventually become Spain's first provincial leader. They were finally on their way to Spain, reaching Salamanca and then Valladolid, where they spent many weeks among the court of Prince Philip and his new Portuguese wife, the daughter of King John III.

Like Faber, Araoz preached at court. Faber also heard confessions, said many Masses, and directed men and women in the Exercises. He would also, over the next months, visit Madrid, Toledo, and Ocaña, in the province of Toledo. However, both men had witnessed what took place in Portugal when provincial Simão Rodrigues became too attached to King John's court, almost forgetting his vows as a Jesuit, leading Araoz to write to Ignatius back in Rome that no Jesuit should ever again reside in a royal court.[148]

# 19

## Finally on the Road to Trent

*[Peter Faber had] simple piety, a certain naïveté.*[149]
—Pope Francis

*He says we should never abandon hope of anyone's reformation.*[150]
—"Teachings of Pierre Favre"

### Late 1545–August 1, 1546

All Western Europe was turned bitter by religious controversy as the middle of the sixteenth century approached. King Francis I of France, with so little sympathy for Protestant heresy, declared in 1535, "If my children were tainted with it, I would myself offer them in sacrifice."[151] It was this king's grandson, Charles IX, who ordered the St. Bartholomew's Day massacre four decades later.

There has been no darker era in human history than the religious wars and theologically inspired hatred that took place across Europe in the decades following Peter Faber's death. Most striking of all was that evening, August 23, 1572, before the feast day of St. Bartholomew the Apostle, when thousands of Protestants (known as Calvinists or Huguenots) were in Paris to celebrate a conciliatory intermarriage between the sister of King Charles IX and Henri of Navarre. With the wedding over but celebrations still under way, Charles IX betrayed the Protestant revelers, who included many of the wealthiest and most powerful people in France, and ordered their slaughter. Assassins killed hundreds that night, and thousands more died the day after. Then, Catholic mob violence spread throughout all France. Eventually as many as seventy thousand people were killed.

There were other instances of this brand of cruelty, and not only in Europe. Puritans in America were attempting to establish theocratic societies. They governed with the Bible, outlawed the practice of any faith but the one they prescribed, and hunted for witches and others perceived to threaten their theocratic and autocratic realm. In England, Dominican inquisitors were employed by the Vatican to hunt for heretics beyond the boundaries of the Holy Roman Empire. In 1542, Pope Paul III established the Congregation of the Holy Office of the Inquisition as a permanent congregation, overseen by cardinals and members of the Curia. The previous century's Spanish Inquisition wasn't the first of its kind, only the first to be organized and well funded, overseen by the royal crown of Spain. That one, as we saw, nearly caught Ignatius of Loyola in its snares before he left to go to school in Paris. Ignatius had made Erasmian friends; he'd studied prayer methods that led some to label him an "illuminist." In fact, he was forbidden to preach for three years in Spain before he left for Paris.

When the Holy Office of the Inquisition was founded in Italy, it was a rechristening. It would be called the Roman Inquisition and found its ideal pope in Paul IV (1555–1559), for Paul IV, when he was Cardinal Gian Pietro Carafa, had been its first inquisitor general. Carafa once said, just like Francis I: "Even if my own father were a heretic, I would gather the wood to burn him."[152] One of our best contemporary historians puts it this way:

> "[He] was one of the nastiest men of the sixteenth century, even by the exacting standards of Reformation and Counter-Reformation nastiness. . . . Paul IV was a good hater, and his hatreds ranged from the trivial to the profoundly important. He hated nudity in art. He hated Jews, and confined the Jewish communities of the Papal States for the first time to ghettos and made them wear distinctive yellow hats. He hated the independent spirit of the Jesuits, and . . . began remodeling them into a more conventional religious order."[153]

This, too, was just a few years after Faber's death.

Pope Paul IV turned against the *Spirituali* who had supported the early Society of Jesus, including Cardinal Contarini, who a decade earlier had convinced Paul III to approve the young order. Contarini died under house arrest, as ordered by Paul IV, and Cardinal Reginald Pole was accused of heresy by the new pope.[154] This was only the beginning. The Roman Inquisition would last for half a century.

The situation between Catholics and Protestants was getting worse and worse as Faber's life came to its close. Statesman and philosopher Michel de Montaigne recalls, in his father's house near Bordeaux, "This was when the innovations of Luther were beginning to gain favor and to shake our old belief in many places." Montaigne remembers how his father's generation viewed this shake-up, "rightly foreseeing . . . that this incipient malady would easily degenerate into an execrable atheism. For the common herd . . . let themselves be carried away . . . when once they have been given the temerity to despise and judge the opinions that they had held in extreme reverence, such as are those in which their salvation is concerned."[155]

Four years after the failed Diet of Regensburg, Luther published his vitriolic tract *Against the Roman Papacy: An Institution of the Devil.* The title says it all. It spread the worst sort of lies about Pope Paul III, including some that would make the most hate-filled twenty-first-century politician blush and would, by today's standards, lead to an enormous libel suit.

Faber began his final year, 1546, worrying as usual about his faults. His daily Examen seemed to never fail to reveal sins and faults to work on. He wrote this at the end of his journal, before leaving Spain for the Council of Trent: "During the first few days of the new year I have experienced a revival of my defects so that I am beginning to get to know them in a new way towards a new amendment. . . . Especially was I now seeing my need of more silence and more solitude."[156]

Maybe he was thinking of the life of his Carthusian friends in Cologne or his own imagined future, but Faber would have little of that solitude in his lifetime.

Pope Paul III's churchwide council had started a month earlier, in December 1545. It was a final attempt to redefine the church in a way that would include, yet minimize, the objections of preachers like Luther. They convened in the alpine town of Trent in the far north of Italy. Paul III had been asking for this council for eight years. It had been postponed three times. During that time, Luther wrote a series of articles declaring the issues upon which he and others couldn't possibly agree with the Catholic establishment. Still, there was hope, and the pope elicited the support of the Flemish Holy Roman Emperor, Charles V, who was still a mediating force. Ignatius thought Faber should be there.

Faber left Spain on April 20, 1546. A few weeks earlier, he'd only partially recovered from an illness, perhaps a stroke, which left him lame in one hand. He felt weak. Rome was only a little out of the way for him as he traveled slowly toward Trent, and, stopping to see his old friend and religious superior, Faber and Ignatius prepared to meet and discuss their concerns for the council. Faber was ill with fever at the time. As he considered the last leg of the journey to come, north through the Papal States, he realized that he was ultimately too sick to travel.

On August 1, 1546, held in the arms of Iñigo, Faber died. His remains lie at rest today near the entrance to the Church of the Gesù, the mother church of the Society of Jesus. Recent Jesuit scholars have estimated that Faber traveled at least seven thousand miles in the last seven years of his life, and then, "to add unrecorded journeys to the twists and turns of the road would surely double that total."[157]

## Meanwhile in Trent

In the months to come at the Council of Trent, the church formally condemned Protestantism and Protestant leaders as heretical, while clarifying Catholic teaching, authority, and territory. They discussed many other matters, as well.

Delegates affirmed a vision of religious knowledge keeping with what was taught by Thomas Aquinas. All three—reason, text, and church tradition—they said, must be brought equally and fully to bear in order to arrive at anything close to truth:

> [N]o one, relying on his personal judgment in matters of faith and customs which are linked to the establishment of Christian doctrine, shall dare to interpret the sacred scriptures either by twisting its text to his individual meaning in opposition to that which has been and is held by holy mother Church, whose function is to pass judgment on the true meaning and interpretation of the sacred scriptures; or by giving it meanings contrary to the unanimous consent of the fathers.[158]

This is an opinion that Faber would have agreed with.

In April and June of the first session, they defended the authority of the Scriptures and the doctrine of original sin. Starting again in January the following year (1547), the hot-button issues of the Reformation were addressed and Catholic doctrine reaffirmed on justification and the essential efficacy of the sacraments. Again, Faber would have felt at home.

But there were other declarations from Trent that would have saddened Faber. From the start, Pope Paul III "had for all practical purposes given up hope of reconciliation with the Reformers. The Lutherans were to be condemned, and, with little more ado, the council could quickly conclude its business."[159]

There were four Jesuits present: Diego Laínez, Alfonso Salmerón, and Claude Jay (Peter's student friend from the Savoy), whom Ignatius sent at Pope Paul III's instructions, and then Peter Canisius, who arrived later, replacing Faber. In the spring of 1543, the Dutch Canisius had traveled to Mainz to find Faber, where Faber guided him through the Exercises. Before Faber's death, Ignatius had instructed the companions who were going with a letter written from Rome. He told them to listen much and speak little and to live out the Jesuit charism in order to support the work of the council:

1. For the greater glory of God our Lord, our main purpose during this stay at Trent is, while trying to live together in some decent place, to preach, hear confessions, and give lectures while teaching children,

giving good example, visiting the poor in hospitals, and exhorting our neighbors—according as each one possesses this or that talent for moving all the persons we can to devotion and prayer, so that they and we may all implore God our Lord that his Divine Majesty will deign to infuse his divine Spirit into all those handling the matters of this high assembly, so that the Holy Spirit may descend upon the council with a greater abundance of gifts and graces.

2. In preaching, I would not touch upon any points where Protestants differ from Catholics; I would merely exhort to virtuous living and to the Church's devotions, urging souls to thorough self-knowledge and to greater knowledge and love of their Creator and Lord. I would frequently mention the council and, as indicated above, conclude each sermon with a prayer for it.[160]

Suspended by Pope Paul IV in the spring of 1547, the Council of Trent was revived again by Julius III in 1551 at the continued urging of Holy Roman Emperor Charles V (understood then as the "Protector of the Church"), who wanted to use the council and his league with the pope as aid in his fight with King Henry II of France. Little happened under Julius III. Trent was revived for a third time by Pope Pius IV in January 1562 with a precise agenda. The gathering would this time more firmly entrench the Catholic Church in opposition to its Protestant cousins. Less than a year after the final session, on November 13, 1564, came the new doctrine and creed of the Catholic Church as the exclusive source of salvation for all people. To find eternal rest in heaven was to be a member of the Roman Catholic Church. As one modern Jesuit historian has put it, "The pope made swearing to it binding on all priests and teachers, an obligation that remained in force into the twentieth century."[161]

# 20

# Interlude: "Take care, take care, that you never close your heart."

Also from *Memoriale*, the teaching "Take care, take care, that you never close your heart" reflects how Faber tried to apply the Gospel of Christ in a simple, yet astonishingly difficult, way. The sentence ultimately came to define his life.

To remind him along the way, Faber believed that he walked and talked each day with angels, watching over him, and saints, praying for him. They were his coaches as he tried to carry this out in daily life.

When he met people, his disposition was one of openness, as expressed in this simple statement: "Never close your heart to anyone," he writes, in the context of relationships with those who disagreed with him. This is of course incredibly difficult to do in everyday life, no less now than in the sixteenth century.

On another occasion, he writes in *Memoriale* about some uneasy feelings he had about certain people. He doesn't refer to them by name, even in the private quiet of his journaling, but clearly he is concerned that his commitment to charity and openness is under threat. On this occasion, his famous devotion to the saints and angels was enforced in what he received interiorly from God: "Seek . . . genuine devotion to God and his saints, and you will easily discover how to deal with your neighbor, be he friend or enemy." He also heard, on this occasion, the admonition "Don't narrow your heart toward God or his concerns."[162]

We see Faber practicing this kind of piety in his prayers for those whom most of his fellow Catholics quickly dismissed as heretics and betrayers of the faith. But again and again, Faber refused to make judgments. He maintained his zeal for mercy to the end. He listened. He kept believing that everyone had the potential to renew their faith, to come back. He didn't close his heart.

# 21

## What Might Have Been

*If only the politicians could hear you! They measure any action by its success. "Does it succeed? Then it's right."*[163]
—Pope John Paul I, from a letter to St. Francis de Sales

*When you tread the ground, fear hell lying beneath it; when you look at the heavens, sigh for the happiness that is there.*[164]
—Peter Faber

One wonders what might have happened in the Catholic Church and the world had Faber been able to do what he saw needed to be done. What if his approach of friendship, conversation, gentleness, and mercy had prevailed? In a letter dispatched to one of the Catholic delegates at the Council of Trent, posted March 7, just before Faber left on this final journey, he offered advice as to the best approach in dealing with Protestants. His first principle was this:

> Anyone wanting to help the heretics of this age must be careful to have great charity for them and to love them in truth, banishing from his soul all considerations which would tend to chill his esteem for them.

The second was this:

> We need to win their goodwill, so that they will love us and accord us a good place in their hearts. We must establish communion in what unites us before doing so in what might evince differences of opinion.

Peter's approach was filial, sincere, and loving. Relationships were what faith was about for him, and every relationship was more important than a fine point of theological argument. But Europe was embroiled in a kind of bitterness that centered on orthodoxy and fear.

While Faber was dying in Rome on August 1, 1546, his old friend Francis Xavier was still traveling on the other side of the world. Xavier hadn't seen Faber and Ignatius for years—and he wouldn't ever again set eyes on them. In September 1552, after his work in India was done, while traveling to China from Japan, Xavier developed a fever that quickly laid him low. Landing on the island of Shangchuan (or São João, Portuguese for "Saint John") eight miles off the southern coast of China in the South China Sea, he died quickly, in a hut on the beach, without friends nearby.

Ignatius received word of Xavier's death months later. He'd written to Xavier weeks earlier, a letter that obviously went unanswered. Ignatius then died too, also of fever (malaria was common in those days), in the Roman summer of 1556. The founding era of the Society of Jesus had come to a close.

Ironically and unfortunately, the history of the Council of Trent is usually divided into three distinct periods: 1545–1549, 1551–1552, and 1562–1563. Protestant leaders like Melanchthon had been urged by Charles V to come to Trent (Melanchthon started to go but then turned around) for that second session, but they wouldn't. They learned that they wouldn't be allowed to vote. The tone had already turned irrevocably. The entire third session was then taken up with a series of condemnations of Protestant principles on divisive points such as the role of the sacraments, the doctrine of justification, and attitudes toward holy orders and ordination.

Faber's Jesuits became the engine that drove the church after Trent. They gave birth to congregations and colleges all over Europe that put into practice the conclusions of the council. The Blessed Virgin Mary was their patron, and frequent Masses became the norm, so much so that the term *communicants* came into existence to describe them.[165] Within the Society of Jesus, administration and doctrinal definition also became more intense after Faber's death. One historian of the order has put it this way, speaking of the Jesuit document that approximates to what is more commonly called a rule in other religious orders: "The Formula of 1540 indicated the purpose of the Society as 'the propagation of the faith and the progress of souls in Christian life and doctrine.' In the version of 1550, the first phrase was significantly expanded to read 'the defense and propagation of the faith.'"[166]

Reform—both the ideas for reform and the word itself—ceased to be used by the Catholic Church after Trent. "Protestants had coopted the word and the need for reform."[167] The next worldwide council wouldn't take place for three more centuries, with Vatican I and its still-controversial definition of papal infallibility, which was essentially the church's continued response to the tumult started back in the Reformation: separation of church from state, representative forms of government, and challenges to papal authority.

After the Council of Trent, Catholic churches moved from a posture of defensiveness to one of boldness. For instance, where Protestants were focusing on making Scripture, art, and even God more accessible and described in the vernacular, the post-Trent Catholic Church emphasized the spectacular: "With the Jesuits in the vanguard, churches and other religious buildings were to be ablaze with light, clouded with incense, draped in lace, smothered in gilt, with huge altars, splendid vestments, sonorous organs and vast choirs, and a liturgy purged of medieval nonsense but essentially triumphalist in its content and amplitude."[168] In other words, access was limited.

After Faber's death, the approach to the Protestant problem changed in both the Society of Jesus and the Catholic Church. The above are just a few examples.

And then there was again the violence. As Peter lay dying in Rome, his mind probably returned to the city he loved: Paris. The schism in the church that he had spent fifteen years experiencing and trying to prevent was in contrast to the firsthand experience of God he'd come to know in his own life. How sad he would have been to see what would happen in Paris between

Protestants and Catholics in the decades to come. In the years after Trent, most European cities saw violence between Protestants and Catholics, including the already mentioned St. Bartholomew's Day massacre in Paris in 1572.

A generation later, Ferdinand II, scion of the House of Hapsburg, attempted to impose Roman Catholicism on all his German subjects. Influenced by strong Jesuit priests, Ferdinand made Catholicism mandatory in his territories, ordered the burning of Protestant books, and closed Protestant churches, exiling all who refused to convert. He mandated that no one may hold office of any kind if he was not willing to make allegiance to the pope.

Beginning in 1618, one calamity followed another, beginning when Ferdinand sent two representatives to Prague to quell the anger of a Protestant majority among the nobles there. Those men were unceremoniously thrown out a second-story window. This sparked what would come to be known as the Thirty Years' War. Northern territories or states joined what came to be known as the Protestant Union, and southern territories or states formed what was called the Catholic League. In the course of three decades, Denmark and Norway banded together to fight against imperial Catholicism, wanting their countries to remain Lutheran. Catholic Spain took the opportunity to go to war with the Protestant Netherlands, since Dutch rebels had been threatening Spanish rule for decades. And France—an overwhelmingly Catholic nation—took the side of the Protestant nations, simply to stick it to the Hapsburgs, whom they already hated. Soon, it was the Swedes' turn to fight against Hapsburg Catholicism, and they mostly succeeded, resulting finally, in 1648, in the Peace of Westphalia, bringing an end to the worst religious war (or series of wars) in the history of Europe. As many as ten million people died, and for what?

The Italian author Roberto Calasso recently wrote, "In the face of mass graves, history returns to being natural history."[169] In other words, intellectual history and religious history no longer matter in the face of these horrors. They have failed.

Peter Faber was a failure by most of the standards we use to judge such things. He was not a success in the way that the world judges successes. His full legacy lies hidden still. It was lost in what he couldn't accomplish. But when you come to know him, in part because of those failures, you begin to recognize the saint whom Pope Francis recently named.

Faber might have kept the church from splitting five hundred years ago. His vision of reform never deviated from his Christian commitments to brotherhood, inclusion, spiritual transformation, and, most of all, mercy. His dedication to kindness and his gentle approach to even disputatious matters of faith went largely unappreciated during his time. Had he lived and had more influence, there may never have been a complete Protestant Reformation. He might have saved us from wars in Europe that claimed too many lives.

This is a tragic story, but it is also a beautiful one. Sometimes the quiet, unassuming man is just as important as the one who makes history. Faber was the man behind other more charismatic men. No one looked up when Faber began to speak in a café, but today, we might wish they had.

In a massive work of Jesuit history written in the half century after Faber's death, one of the priests who knew him well summarized his life this way: "There was an especially rare and delightful sweetness and charm in his relations with other men which I must confess to this very day I have not discovered in any other. In some way or other, he so won the friendship of other men and gradually stole into their souls that by his whole manner and the gentleness of his words he irresistibly drew them to a love of God."[170]

Pope Francis summarized Faber's spiritual genius as "dialogue with all, even the most remote and even with his opponents." He listed his most remarkable qualities in the tradition of that earlier characterization: "simple piety, a certain naïveté perhaps, his being available straightaway, his careful interior discernment, the fact that he was a man capable of great and strong decisions but also capable of being so gentle and loving."[171] These are qualities that were rare in his day and remain uncommon in ours. One wonders what the modern world might have been like had Faber's way of being faithful endured.

Pope Francis has said: "We need to seek God in order to find him, and find him in order to seek him again and always. Peter Faber was a restless, unsettled, spirit that was never satisfied." If there is one reason Jesuits have long regarded Faber as their favorite Jesuit saint, turning to him as much as or more than his famous friends, it is Peter's humility. Superior general Adolfo Nicolás, SJ, summarized Faber's gift for "pedagogy in a soft voice" after the canonization.[172] Pope Francis praises Faber's restlessness, his dreaming, and his desire to change the world. "Here is the question we must ask ourselves: do we also have great vision? Are we also daring? Does zeal consume us?" Francis asks.

We are to continue the story of Faber in our own lives.

# The Encore:
# Prayers of St. Peter Faber

*Remember that all our failures are ultimately failures in love.*
—Iris Murdoch, *The Bell*

## A Prayer for Discernment

I beg of you, my Lord,
to remove anything that separates
me from you, and you from me.
Remove anything that makes me unworthy
of your sight, your control, your reprehension;
of your speech and conversation,
of your benevolence and love

Take from me every evil
that stands in the way of my seeing you,
hearing, tasting, savoring, and touching you;
fearing and being mindful of you;
knowing, trusting, loving, and possessing you;
being conscious of your presence
and, as far as may be, enjoying you.
This is what I ask for myself
and earnestly desire from you.
Amen.

## To the Holy Spirit

Spirit of God, please
protect and defend me.
  Be my being, my life,
my senses, and my mind
against every wicked spirit
and every evil.

## For Reconciliation

Good Lord Jesus, allow the sins we commit
not to hurt the community of which we are a part.
We have sinned against you; we have hampered the
salvation of our souls; and we have done little to
help the salvation of others.
We deserve punishments and corrections.
But don't, we pray, remember these sins, and
please don't allow them to stand in the way of our
growth as a holy community dedicated to your name.
Amen.[173]

## Prayer for Receiving the Eucharist

I see this Host before me, the Body of God, just as
John the Baptist saw Jesus coming to him by the river,
saying, "Behold the Lamb of God who takes away the
sins of the world." Amen.[174]

## For Improving in Prayer

Heavenly Father,
give me your good spirit.[175]

## Prayer of Desire to Sense Christ's Presence

Holy and mysterious God,

teach me to praise and honor you, O Christ,

to think about and know you,

to remember and long for you,

to love and desire and serve you,

to seek and see and hear you,

to know your fragrance, to delight in you,

to touch you.

Amen.[176]

## A Priest's Prayer after Administering the Sacrament

I hope you will grant, Lord, that I might give what I have

offered, and that I might belong to everyone.

Make me Your instrument, that I may not only belong to all,

but live and work, for and on behalf of, all.

May I be present, as priest, for the praise of You and the

salvation of every soul, alive and dead,

according to Your will. Amen.[177]

## Prayer for Vocations
(Prayed while he was in Germany surveying the religious landscape)

God, send us enough vocations to help transform this troubled world!

We need people, both lay and ordained, willing to live lives of

obedience.

Please send us people who can discern spirits.

Please send us people of faith, hope, and love—

so that we may restore the glory of your Church.

Amen.[178]

# Notes

1. From "Teachings of Pierre Favre as Recorded by the Prior of the Cologne Carthusians, Gerhard Kalckbrenner" (Faber's friend and colleague), in *The Spiritual Writings of Pierre Favre*, eds. Edmond C. Murphy, SJ, and John W. Padberg, SJ, trans. Edmond C. Murphy, SJ and Martin E. Palmer, SJ (St. Louis, MO: Institute of Jesuit Sources, 1996), 385.

2. Pope Francis, homily, Church of the Gesù, Rome, January 3, 2014. http://www.vatican.va/content/francesco/en/homilies/2014/documents/papa-francesco_20140103_omelia-santissimo-nome-gesu.html.

3. John Patrick Donnelly, SJ, ed. and trans., *Jesuit Writings of the Early Modern Period: 1540–1640* (Indianapolis, IN: Hackett Publishing, 2006).

4. Massimo Firpo, "*The Italian Reformation and Juan de Valdes,*" trans. John Tedeschi, *Sixteenth Century Journal* 27, no. 2 (1996): 353.

5. Antonio Spadaro, SJ, "A Big Heart Open to God: An Interview with Pope Francis," *America*, September 30, 2013, http://www.americamagazine.org/faith/2013/09/30/big-heart-open-god-interview-pope-francis.

6. Pope Francis, homily in Rome, January 3, 2014.

7. From William V. Bangert, SJ, *To the Other Towns: A Life of Blessed Peter Favre, First Companion of Saint Ignatius* (San Francisco, CA: Ignatius Press, 2002), 20.

8. Quoted in *Lytton Strachey: The New Biography*, Michael Holroyd (New York: W.W. Norton, 2005), xxxvi.

9. Here, for the first time but not the last time, I have quoted from the IJS translation of *Memoriale* but changed a word or two. In this case, their "yet" becomes "still," and more importantly, their "conscious" becomes "aware." Murphy and Padberg, eds., *The Spiritual Writings of Pierre Favre* (St. Louis, MO: Institute of Jesuit Sources, 1996), 2, 61. All quotations from *Memoriale* henceforward reference

simply the page number of the 1996 edition—the second of the two numbers in this note. Occasionally I note that the quotation is my paraphrase.

10. Stephen O'Shea, *The Alps: A Human History from Hannibal to "Heidi" and Beyond* (New York: W. W. Norton, 2017), 6–7.

11. See Jean Leclercq, "Saint Bernard's Attitude toward War," in *Studies in Medieval Cistercian History II*, ed. John R. Sommerfeldt (Kalamazoo, MI: Cistercian Publications, 1976).

12. Bangert, *To the Other Towns*, 25.

13. Douay-Rheims, Rom. 8:7, 7:14.

14. Douay-Rheims, Rom. 7:24.

15. *Memoriale*, 4, 62; 5, 63.

16. Ibid., 4, 62.

17. As quoted and translated by Euan K. Cameron in "Ways of Knowing in the Pre- and Post-Reformation Worlds," *Mysticism and Reform: 1400–1750*, ed. Sara S. Poor and Nigel Smith (Notre Dame, IN: University of Notre Dame Press, 2015), 35.

18. Richard F. Lovelace, "Evangelical Spirituality: A Church Historian's Perspective," *Journal of the Evangelical Theological Society* 31, no. 1 (March 1988): 25–35, http://www.etsjets.org/files/JETS-PDFs/31/31-1/31-1-pp025-035_JETS.pdf.

19. My translations, all from the first two pages of chapter 18. See Machiavelli's *The Prince*, trans. Peter Constantine (New York: Modern Library, 2008), 81–82, for comparison.

20. *The Pilgrim's Guide to Santiago de Compostela: A Gazetteer*, trans. Annie Shaver-Crandell and Paula Gerson (London: Harvey Miller Publishers, 1995), 67–68.

21. Chris Wickham, *Medieval Europe* (New Haven, CT: Yale University Press, 2016), 122.

22. From his homily, January 3, 2014.

23. Guibert of Nogent, as quoted in Leclercq, "Saint Bernard's Attitude toward War," 5.

24. Katy Gibbons, *English Catholic Exiles in Late Sixteenth-Century Paris* (Rochester, NY: Royal Historical Society/Boydell Press, 2011), 75.

25. Diarmaid MacCulloch, *All Things Made New: The Reformation and Its Legacy* (New York: Oxford University Press, 2016), 82.

26. Simone Roux, *Paris in the Middle Ages*, trans. Jo Ann McNamara (Philadelphia: University of Pennsylvania Press, 2011), 110.

27. As quoted in Tanya Stabler Miller, *The Beguines of Medieval Paris: Gender, Patronage, and Spiritual Authority* (Philadelphia: University of Pennsylvania Press, 2018), 88.

28. Carlos M. N. Eire, *From Madrid to Purgatory: The Art and Craft of Dying in Sixteenth-Century Spain* (New York: Cambridge University Press, 2002), 515.

29. Friedrich Heer, *The Intellectual History of Europe*, Vol. 2, *The Counter-Reformation to 1945*, trans. Jonathan Steinberg (Garden City, NY: Anchor Books, 1968), 2.

30. Mary Purcell, *The First Jesuit* (Westminster, MD: Newman Press, 1957), 22–23.

31. As quoted by Martin Brecht in *Martin Luther*, trans. James L. Schaaf (Philadelphia: Fortress Press, 1985), 1:460.

32. Quotes taken from *Reminiscences*, I.2, Penguin ed., p. 13.

33. Ibid., I.4, Penguin ed., p. 15.

34. Ibid., I.7, I.1, Penguin ed., pp. 15, 13.

35. Jacobus de Voragine, *The Golden Legend: Readings on the Saints*, trans. William Granger Ryan (Princeton, NJ: Princeton University Press, 2012), 244.

36. Diarmaid MacCulloch, *Christianity: The First Three Thousand Years* (New York: Penguin Books, 2011), 556.

37. Andrew Pettegree, *The Book in the Renaissance* (New Haven, CT: Yale University Press, 2011), 91–92.

38. We know also that "between 1498 and 1650, at least 750 separate editions of the Book of Revelation, and commentaries on it, were published, many of them in convenient and cheap editions." Andrew Cunningham and Ole Peter Grell, *The Four Horsemen of the Apocalypse: Religion, War, Famine and Death in Reformation Europe* (New York: Cambridge University Press, 2000), 4.

39. Ferdinand Addis, *The Eternal City: A History of Rome* (New York: Pegasus Books, 2018), 434.

40. Henri-Jean Martin, *The French Book: Religion, Absolutism, and Readership, 1585–1715*, trans. Paul Saenger and Nadine Saenger (Baltimore: Johns Hopkins University Press, 1996), 12.

41. See *Reminiscences*, mostly I.21, Penguin ed., p. 22.

42. Joanot Martorell and Marti Joan de Galba, *Tirant lo Blanc*, ed. David H. Rosenthal (Baltimore: Johns Hopkins University Press, 1996), 3–4.

43. Mark Kurlansky, *The Basque History of the World: The Story of a Nation* (New York: Penguin Books, 2001), 76.

44. Roux, *Paris in the Middle Ages*, (University of Pennsylvania Press, 2009), 111, 81.

45. Francis Xavier, *The Life and Letters of St. Francis Xavier, Vol. 1*, ed. Henry James Coleridge (London: Burns & Oates, 1881), https://archive.org/stream/lifelettersofstf01coleuoft/lifelettersofstf01coleuoft_djvu.txt.

46. Michael A. Mullett, *Martin Luther*, 2nd ed. (New York: Routledge, 2015), 86.

47. Aristotle, *The Nicomachean Ethics*, trans. David Ross (New York: Oxford University Press, 1980), VIII, 1; 192–93.

48. Ibid., 196–7.

49. Samuel Taylor Coleridge, *Biographia Literaria*, ed. James Engell and W. Jackson Bate (Princeton, NJ: Princeton University Press, 1983), 1:241–42.

50. *Memoriale*, 8, 64.

51. Ibid. I have rendered these quotations more freely than in Murphy.

52. As he records of himself in *Reminiscences*, II.18, Penguin ed., p. 20.

53. W. W. Meissner, SJ, MD, *Ignatius of Loyola: The Psychology of a Saint* (New Haven, CT: Yale University Press, 1992), 150.

54. *Memoriale*, 8, 64.

55. Ibid., 10, 65.

56. This version comes from the Ignatian Spirituality page of resources at the website www.jesuits.org/spirituality?PAGE=DTN-20130520125910.

57. *Memoriale*, 9, 65. The second quote is my freer rendering.

58. Thomas Aquinas, from "Soul in Human Beings," in *Selected Philosophical Writings*, trans. Timothy McDermott (New York: Oxford University Press, 1993), 190.

59. Barton T. Geger, SJ, "A Word from the Editor," *Studies in the Spirituality of Jesuits* 49, no. 2 (Summer 2017): iii–iv.

60. Sean Salai, SJ, "What do Graham Greene, Flannery O'Connor and Caravaggio have in common? Their Ignatian imagination," *America*, December 21, 2016.

https://www.americamagazine.org/arts-culture/2016/12/21/
what-do-graham-greene-flannery-oconnor-and-caravaggio-have-common-their.

61. René Fülöp-Miller, *The Power and Secret of the Jesuits* (1930; rpt., n.p., CreateSpace, 2014), 415.

62. *Memoriale*, 2, 61. This is my rendering.

63. See O'Shea, *The Alps*, 262–63.

64. *Memoriale*, 14, 67.

65. Antonio Spadaro, SJ, *A Big Heart Open to God: A Conversation with Pope Francis* (New York: HarperOne, 2013), 20.

66. *Saint Ignatius of Loyola: Personal Writings*, trans. Joseph A. Munitiz and Philip Endean (New York: Penguin Books, 2004), 29, 33.

67. Letter of instructions to Jesuits about to go on pilgrimage, dated spring 1543, in *The Spiritual Writings of Pierre Favre*, 340–41.

68. George E. Ganss, SJ, *The Spiritual Exercises of Saint Ignatius: A Translation and Commentary* (Chicago: Loyola Press, 1992), SE 315, 121.

69. Martin Luther, *Luther's Works*, 55 vols., ed. Jaroslav Pelikan and H. T. Lehmann (St. Louis, MO: Concordia, 1955–1986), 40:117.

70. See *Summa Theologiae*, IIaIIae, q. 2, art. 3.

71. Voltaire, *Treatise on Toleration*, trans. Desmond M. Clarke (New York: Penguin, 2016), 29.

72. Eusebius, *Life of Constantine*, in *The Church and the Roman Empire (301–490): Constantine, Councils, and the Fall of Rome*, Mike Aquilina (Notre Dame, IN: Ave Maria Press, 2019), 44.

73. *Memoriale*, 14, 67.

74. See Joseph Conwell, *Contemplation in Action: A Study in Ignatian Prayer* (Spokane, WA: Gonzaga University Press, 1957), 23–39.

75. Michel de Montaigne, from the essay, "Of the useful and the honorable." *The Complete Essays of Montaigne*, trans. Donald M. Frame (Stanford, CA: Stanford University Press, 1968), 599.

76. John W. O'Malley, *The First Jesuits* (Cambridge, MA: Harvard University Press, 1993), 32.

77. *Memoriale*, 8, 64–65.

78. *St. Justin Martyr: Dialogue with Trypho*, trans. Thomas B. Falls, revised by Thomas P. Halton, ed. Michael Slusser (Washington, DC: Catholic University of America Press, 2003), 1, 4.

79. O'Malley, *The First Jesuits*, 12.

80. Friedrich Heer, *The Intellectual History of Europe*, Vol. 2, *The Counter-Reformation to 1945*, trans. Jonathan Steinberg (New York: Anchor Books, 1968), 25.

81. *Meditations on the Life of Christ: An Illustrated Manuscript of the Fourteenth Century*, trans. Isa Ragusa, ed. Isa Ragusa and Rosalie B. Green (Princeton, NJ: Princeton University Press, 1961), 103–4.

82. James Martin, SJ, *The Jesuit Guide to (Almost) Everything: A Spirituality for Real Life* (New York: HarperOne, 2012), 239–40.

83. The depiction of a humiliated Christian tradition in this paragraph is derived, in large part, from the twentieth-century Jesuit philosopher Michel de Certeau's introduction to *The Mystic Fable: The Sixteenth and Seventeenth Centuries, Vol. 1*, trans. Michael B. Smith (Chicago: University of Chicago Press, 1992), 25.

84. *Memoriale*, 16, 71 (and the quote that follows this one).

85. O'Malley, *The First Jesuits*, 34, 315.

86. Bangert, *To the Other Towns*, 61.

87. *Saint Ignatius of Loyola: Personal Writings*, 145.

88. Alex Bamji, "Medical Care in Early Modern Venice" (Economic History Working Paper No. 188), London School of Economics and Political Science, London, 2014, 9–10, http://www.lse.ac.uk/economicHistory/workingPapers/2014/WP188.pdf.

89. *Saint Ignatius of Loyola: Personal Writings*, 145.

90. O'Malley, *The First Jesuits*, 33–34.

91. Ibid., 92.

92. *The Spiritual Writings of Pierre Favre*, 70.

93. *Memoriale*, 18, 72, my rendering.

94. John W. O'Malley, SJ, "How the First Jesuits Became Involved in Education," in *The Jesuit Ratio Studiorum: 400th Anniversary Perspectives*, ed. Vincent J. Duminuco, SJ (New York: Fordham University Press, 2000), 60.

95. Quoted in Laurence Bergreen, *Over the Edge of the World: Magellan's Terrifying Circumnavigation of the Globe* (New York: Harper Perennial, 2004), 32.

96. Caius Plinius Secundus, *Naturalis Historia* (Natural History), II.72.

97. *Memoriale*, 18, 72.

98. Ibid., 19, 73. This quotation and the one that follows it are both my renderings.

99. This letter is in ibid., 319–20.

100. MacCulloch, *All Things Made New*, 1.

101. *The Way: A Review of Christian Spirituality Published by the British Jesuits* 56, no. 4 (October 2017).

102. J. H. Plumb, *The Italian Renaissance*, rev. ed. (New York: Mariner Books, 2001), 99.

103. Quoted by Lyndal Roper in *Martin Luther: Renegade and Prophet* (London: Bodley Head, 2016), 381.

104. From January 16, 1545; see *The Spiritual Writings of Pierre Favre*, 287. This is also the source for the brief quotations that appear two paragraphs later in the text.

105. *The Spiritual Writings of Pierre Favre*, 379.

106. Ibid., 97.

107. Michel de Certeau, from "Mystic Speech," in *Heterologies: Discourse on the Other*, trans. Brian Massumi (Minneapolis: University of Minnesota Press, 1985), 80.

108. O'Malley, *The First Jesuits*, 16. Speaking of the Jesuit attitude toward the Reformation.

109. *Saint Ignatius of Loyola: Personal Writings*, 169.

110. *Memoriale*, in *The Spiritual Writings*, 74.

111. *The Spiritual Writings*, 75–76.

112. Ibid., 78–79.

113. Ibid., 79.

114. Ibid., 80.

115. Ibid., 84–85.

116. See July 17, 1542, in *The Spiritual Writings*, 95.

117. See *The Spiritual Writings*, 102.

118. Ibid., 104.

119. Letter of instructions to Jesuits about to go on pilgrimage, dated spring 1543, in *The Spiritual Writings*, 341.

120. Letter to Ignatius of Loyola, April 27, 1542, in *The Spiritual Writings*, 335.

121. From "Teachings of Pierre Favre," in *The Spiritual Writings*, 387.

122. *The Spiritual Writings*, 118–19.

123. From June 21, 1543, in *The Spiritual Writings*, 257.

124. Their "robust" does not seem to convey as well as "strong" Peter's feelings of desire. *The Spiritual Writings*, 60.

125. Letter to Ignatius of Loyola, dated April 27, 1542, in *The Spiritual Writings*, 333–34.

126. *The Spiritual Writings*, 153.

127. *Memoriale*, 63.

128. *The Spiritual Writings*, 161.

129. Ibid., 249.

130. *Memoriale*, 12. My translation.

131. See *The Spiritual Writings*, 176.

132. See December 1542 writings in *The Spiritual Writings*, 182.

133. *The Spiritual Writings*, 204.

134. Ibid., 192.

135. Ibid.

136. See *Memoriale* for January 7, 1542, for all of this, in *The Spiritual Writings*, 195–98. This is mostly by paraphrasing. The one quotation in quotation marks is from 195–96.

137. *The Spiritual Writings*, 230.

138. About vocabulary, see ibid., 238. The quotation is my paraphrase. About the crucifixes in Mainz, see ibid., 245.

139. From June 1543, see ibid., 256.

140. These bits of renewal and advice are mentioned in a letter to Carthusian Gerhard Kalckbrenner in April 1543, in *The Spiritual Writings*, 344–45.

141. Murphy and Padberg, editorial note, in *The Spiritual Writings*, 273.

142. *The Spiritual Writings*, 278.

143. Letter from 1553, in *Saint Ignatius of Loyola: Personal Writings*, 252.

144. References to epistles 82 and 80, as the letters are cataloged by scholars. See *Memoriale*, 356, 354.

145. Epistle 82, 356–57.

146. Ibid.

147. *The Spiritual Writings*, 365; the full letter is at 365–67.

148. O'Malley, *The First Jesuits*, 149.

149. Spadaro, "A Big Heart Open to God."

150. *The Spiritual Writings*, 386.

151. Quoted in Benjamin J. Kaplan, *Divided Faith: Religious Conflict and the Practice of Toleration in Early Modern Europe* (Cambridge, MA: Belknap Press of Harvard University Press, 2007), 1.

152. Quoted in Addis, *The Eternal City*, 436.

153. MacCulloch, *All Things Made New*, 83.

154. O'Malley, *The First Jesuits*, 316.

155. *The Complete Essays of Montaigne*, 320.

156. *The Spiritual Writings*, 314.

157. Murphy and Padberg in *The Spiritual Writings*, 31.

158. *Decrees of the Ecumenical Councils*, 2 vols., ed. and trans. Norman P. Tanner (Washington, DC: Georgetown University Press, 1990), 664. The two volumes are paginated consecutively.

159. John W. O'Malley, *Trent: What Happened at the Council* (Cambridge, MA: Harvard University Press, 2013), 13.

160. John W. Padberg et al., eds., *Ignatius of Loyola: Letters and Instructions* (St. Louis, MO: Institute of Jesuit Sources, 1996), 129–30.

161. O'Malley, *Trent*, 262.

162. *The Spiritual Writings*, 151. The first quote is verbatim; the second is my paraphrase.

163. Albino Luciani, *Illustrissimi: The Letters of Pope John Paul I*, preface by Cardinal Basil Hume (London: Collins/Fount, 1979), 129.

164. Faber, from the summary of his teachings by Gerhard Kalckbrenner; see *The Spiritual Writings*, 390.

165. Louis Chatellier, *The Europe of the Devout: The Catholic Reformation and the Formation of a New Society* (New York: Cambridge University Press, 1989), 3–4.

166. O'Malley, *The First Jesuits*, 5.

167. John W. O'Malley, *Vatican I: The Council and the Making of the Ultramontane Church* (Cambridge, MA: Harvard University Press, 2018), 4.

168. Paul Johnson, *The Renaissance: A Short History* (New York: Modern Library, 2000), 185–86.

169. Roberto Calasso, *The Ruin of Kasch*, trans. Richard Dixon (New York: Farrar, Straus & Giroux, 2018), 7.

170. From the sixteenth-century *Monumenta Borgia*, translated here by William V. Bangert, SJ, in *To the Other Towns*, 36.

171. Pope Francis, "A Big Heart Open to God: an Interview with Pope Francis," *America*, September 30, 2013.

172. A letter to his fellow Jesuits, from Rome, December 17, published in *Ignis: Ignatian Spirituality Quarterly* (Gujarat, India) 44, no. 1 (2014): 50.

173. My rendering of a prayer recorded in Faber's *Memoriale* on January 21, 1545. See *The Spiritual Writings*, 289.

174. My rendering, slightly expanding on a prayer Faber records in his *Memoriale* as one he would offer to the laity while distributing the Eucharist at Mass. See *The Spiritual Writings*, 284.

175. This is verbatim from *The Spiritual Writings*, 81.

176. This prayer is stated as an intention to pray by Faber in *Memoriale*, July 21, 1542; *The Spiritual Writings*, 96. I have only slightly paraphrased the language.

177. This prayer is my paraphrase of Faber's intention, and then the words he records of his actual prayer, in section 142 of *Memoriale*, *The Spiritual Writings*, 150.

178. My paraphrase of Faber's intention, including words he records that he prayed, from section 265 of *Memoriale*. See *The Spiritual Writings*, 219–20.

# About the Author

Jon M. Sweeney is an award-winning author and book publisher. He's been interviewed in print by a range of publications from the *Dallas Morning News* to *The Irish Catholic* and on television for *CBS Saturday Morning* and *Fox News*. His 2012 history, *The Pope Who Quit*, was optioned by HBO. He's also the author of thirty other books including *The Complete Francis of Assisi*; *James Martin, SJ*, a biography; and *The Pope's Cat* series for children. He is a Catholic, married to a rabbi, and their interfaith marriage has been profiled in national media. He writes regularly for *America: The Jesuit Review* in the U.S., *The Tablet* in the UK, and occasionally for *The Christian Century*. He is active on social media (Twitter @jonmsweeney; Facebook jonmsweeney), is the publisher at Paraclete Press in Massachusetts, and lives in Milwaukee with his wife and daughters.

# More Books About Jesuit Saints

## THE QUIET COMPANION
### THE LIFE OF PETER FABER, SJ

MARY PURCELL

One of St. Ignatius of Loyola's most trusted companions, Peter Faber worked quietly toward internal reform of the Church and became a pioneer of ecumenism. *The Quiet Companion*, by the noted Irish historian Mary Purcell, outlines the importance of Peter Faber's work and the upheaval of the times in which he lived. Known for being extremely hard on himself but gentle with others, he spent his life working for the renewal of the Church one person at a time.

Paperback | 978-0-8294-4101-7 | $16.95

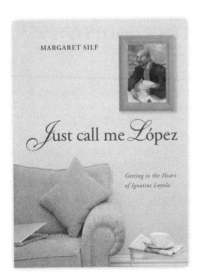

## JUST CALL ME LÓPEZ
### GETTING TO THE HEART OF IGNATIUS LOYOLA

MARGARET SILF

What could we have in common with a man from the sixteenth century? How about a man from the sixteenth century who becomes a saint? In *Just Call Me López*, the story of a twenty-first-century woman, Rachel, who meets Íñigo López—the man we know today as St. Ignatius—is imagined by author Margaret Silf. Both are transformed by their unlikely friendship and series of thought-provoking conversations. *Just Call Me López* helps us realize that our very human faults and imperfect behavior can reveal God within us and the path before us.

Hardcover | 978-0-8294-3668-6 | $14.95

## To Order:
Call **800.621.1008**, visit **store.loyolapress.com**, or visit your local bookseller.

# More Books on Ignatian Spirituality

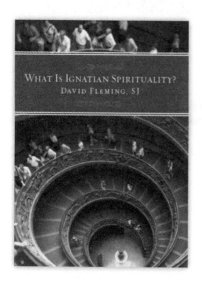

## WHAT IS IGNATIAN SPIRITUALITY?

### DAVID FLEMING, SJ

In *What Is Ignatian Spirituality?* St. Ignatius and the key elements of his teachings are brought to life by David Fleming, SJ. This highly accessible summary of the key elements of the spirituality of St. Ignatius includes a look at contemplative prayer, discernment, and what it means to be actively involved in service and mission.

English: Paperback I 978-0-8294-2718-9 I $12.95
Spanish: Paperback I 978-0-8294-3883-3 I $12.95

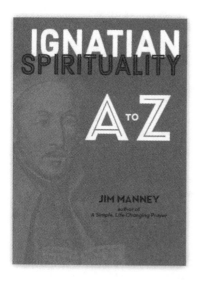

## IGNATIAN SPIRITUALITY A TO Z

### JIM MANNEY

With *Ignatian Spirituality A to Z*, Jim Manney has provided a brief, informative, and entertaining guide to key concepts of Ignatian spirituality and essential characters and events in Jesuit history. The lexicon format allows readers to find terms quickly, and the concise descriptions are ideal for those new to the Ignatian story.

Paperback I 978-0-8294-4598-5 I $14.95

## To Order:

Call **800.621.1008**, visit **store.loyolapress.com**, or visit your local bookseller.